The Oliver Wight ABCD Checklist for Operational Excellence

The Oliver Wight ABCD Checklist for Operational Excellence

FOURTH EDITION

John Wiley & Sons, Inc.
New York · Chichester · Brisbane · Toronto · Singapore

Printed in the United States of America

10 9 8 7

ACKNOWLEDGMENTS

The Oliver Wight ABCD Checklist for Operational Excellence is not authored by one or even a few people. It is a collection of the experiences of people from hundreds of companies compiled over a period of more than fifteen years.

This fourth edition of the checklist is a major update, built on the previous versions developed by Oliver Wight in the 1970s, and a substantial revision to the checklist that was published in 1988 by the team of Walt Goddard, Dick Ling, George Palmatier, John Sari, and myself.

This edition of the ABCD Checklist recognizes the rapid developments in management tools and techniques available to companies today. Its purpose is to expand the role of the checklist as an industry standard for operational performance measurement, thereby helping companies achieve world-class levels of performance.

The development team for this checklist included:

- Tom Wallace, the contributor of the strategic planning material and final editor
- Darryl Landvater, who provided substantial support in his role as Vice President of Products and Technologies for the Oliver Wight organization
- Bill Belgard, Donna Neusch, and Steve Rayner, who created the section on people/team processes

- Bill Boyst, Terry Johnson, George Killianey, and Bill Sandras, who authored the chapter on total quality and Continuous Improvement
- Dale Hiatt, who provided the material on new product development
- Doug Burns, who developed the PC-based version of the checklist
- Pete Landry, George Palmatier, Paul Politte, and John Sari, who reviewed and contributed to the interim versions of this document
- Jerry Clement, Jim Correll, Dick Ling, and Pete Skurla, who did a fine job of critiquing the checklist

Thanks goes also to the people from client companies who participated in the field tests of the checklist. I speak for the team and The Oliver Wight Companies in offering to all of you our sincere thanks. Together we have compiled a set of criteria that a company can use to determine how well it's operating, identify opportunities for improvement, and monitor its progress on the continuous journey to operational excellence.

Steven A. Souza
Assonet, Massachusetts

CONTENTS

INTRODUCTION

Perspective

Are we doing the right things? How well are we doing them? Are we on the right track to world-class performance? It's hard to imagine three more valuable questions for all managers to ask frequently. The answers reflect current levels of performance and reveal significant opportunities for improvement.

Finding the right answers, however, requires many more questions. This checklist raises those questions. As such, it's an important tool in appraising a company's effectiveness in utilizing the many technologies available to manufacturing companies today.

A good checklist does more than tell you where you are today—it helps managers focus on what's required to become more competitive and achieve world-class levels of performance. Periodic use of the checklist generates a consistent means of assessing progress. In addition, it identifies problems early, which allow the correction process to start immediately. Further, by comparing performance against established benchmarks, people are motivated to work in a more effective manner.

Evolution

Ollie Wight created our first ABCD Checklist in 1977. It consisted of twenty items designed to evaluate a Manufacturing Resource Planning system, MRP II. The items were grouped into three categories: technical, to determine whether the design was proper; data accuracy, to determine how reliable the information was; and operational, to determine how well MRP II was understood and used within the company.

A few years later the original list was expanded to twenty-five items. This checklist is the accepted industry standard for measuring MRP II. By responding to these items, a person can objectively grade a company's use of MRP II into one of four categories: A, B, C, or D. These levels of potential have served as challenging goals, especially to reach the Class A level.

No Longer Just MRP II

During the 1980s, the third generation of the ABCD Checklist was created, which was broader in scope. It covered not only operational planning and control processes—MRP II and Distribution Resource Planning (DRP)—but also contained items in the important areas of strategic planning and Continuous Improvement. The third edition also contained entries for both the overview level, to facilitate review by the general manager and staff, and the detail level, to serve as a tool for operating personnel to diagnose and correct deficiencies.

The Fourth Edition of the ABCD Checklist

This new checklist is significantly more comprehensive than its predecessors. For this reason, we've organized the checklist into chapters based on basic business functions. These are:

- Strategic Planning Processes
- People/Team Processes
- Total Quality and Continuous Improvement Processes
- New Product Development Processes
- Planning and Control Processes

It would be an overwhelming task for most companies to attack simultaneously all of these business processes and their underlying technologies. Implementing all of these major changes at the same time would call for too much work to be done by people who already have full-time jobs in running the business.

There are significant risks in trying to do too much at one time: nothing gets done well, people burn out, and competitive advantage is lost.

The chapter organization of this checklist allows a company to choose one or several of these basic business processes and concentrate its energies on that choice. An organization can choose to pursue as much, or as little, as it feels capable of pursuing.

Qualitative Characteristics and Overview Items

Each chapter begins with brief Qualitative Characteristics of the various levels of performance—Class A, B, C, and D—for the processes in question. Then listed are the Overview Items, which provide an executive summary. They're designed to allow executives to evaluate whether necessary processes exist and, if so, how well they are being used.

Detail Items

Following this executive summary, the Detail Items are then spelled out, grouped under their respective Overview Items. These Detail Items provide additional information, guidance, and means for assessment, and make up the main body of the checklist. They're designed to provide operating managers with a tool for assessing the significant characteristics of each process, checking the vital "how tos" of each process, and analyzing in greater detail how well the processes are being used. For most of the Overview Items, several Detail Items are listed that will help determine your position on the scale for each Overview Item. A few Overview Items, however, have no Detail Items, and these are noted in the text with an asterisk (*).

Duplication of Entries

This checklist covers multiple technologies, and there's sometimes overlap from one to another. For example, many of the Overview and

Detail Items involved in effective People/Team Processes are necessary for Total Quality and Continuous Improvement Processes. Therefore, in some cases, it's been necessary to include the same items in more than one chapter. These have been noted in the text with a dagger (†).

Scoring of Responses

In prior editions of the checklist, responses were limited to "yes" or "no" (or, where appropriate, "not applicable").

This new checklist, however, enables responses to be made on a scale of 0 (Not Doing) to 4 (Excellent). This helps in identifying what's been done and what remains to be done, and can serve as an impetus for Continuous Improvement.

Objective

Our objective in publishing *The Oliver Wight ABCD Checklist for Operational Excellence* is to help companies become the best they can be. We hope you find this tool helps you to ask the right questions and determine the right answers to achieve absolute world-class performance, to become truly excellent in all operational aspects of the business. If so, then we have indeed produced a Class A product.

Walter E. Goddard
President
The Oliver Wight Companies

HOW TO USE THE CHECKLIST

The best way to use the checklist is as a vision of what could exist in your company, and pursue it aggressively, systematically, and relentlessly. Companies using the checklist in this way are using it effectively, and are achieving the potential of their organization.

Not all companies use the ABCD Checklist this way. Some companies use the checklist merely as a results indicator in the later stages of an implementation program. While beneficial, this does little to ensure continuing improvement.

For this reason, we recommend following the steps listed below to enable your company to use the checklist to achieve better results both in the short-term and on a sustained basis in the future.

Performance Improvement Process

1. Assess current status
2. Establish goals and objectives
3. Tailor the checklist to your company's immediate needs
4. Develop action plans
5. Measure progress
6. Conduct monthly management reviews

With the ABCD Checklist, the performance improvement process begins with an assessment of the company's current strengths and weaknesses. Many companies start by answering the questions that pertain to their areas of focus. If planning and control systems are an issue for your company, then you might focus only on this chapter. It's not necessary to

5

answer the items in all five chapters. On the other hand, you may choose to address all five chapters to get an overall assessment of the situation in your company. However you choose to use the checklist, remember to answer *all* the questions in each chapter that you select. The only exception to this is when the items are not applicable to your business.

Most companies meet in groups of ten to twenty people to discuss the questions in the checklist. The groups allow for discussion and the comparing of differences. If one person feels the master production schedule is well managed but others can identify specific situations when poorly thought-out changes have been made, then a healthy discussion will take place. It's important to have several levels of management take part in these discussions, normally in several groups. It's typical for things to look better when viewed from the top of the organization.

There are a few prerequisites for these discussions to be useful. The first is that the participants must be knowledgeable. This means being familiar with the terms and techniques that are referenced and having an adequate understanding as to why the processes are important for the company to operate at a very high standard.

Second, it assumes that the answers will come from people of "good intentions." Knowledgeable people who are sincerely attempting to be objective can avoid seeing the world through rose-colored glasses or being overly critical to the extent that any minor imperfection leads to a negative response.

No matter how well phrased the items in this checklist may be, we recognize that degrees of interpretation are required to answer them. We also realize that a significant element of judgment is needed before answering many items. The combination of interpretation and judgment will, hopefully, lead to healthy internal discussion. The checklist will be productive if companies use it to review why these processes are important, what each process consists of, how the process can contribute to improvements, and how to accomplish these improvements.

Scoring the Results

The response to both Overview and Detail Items are scored on a range from "Excellent" to "Not Doing," with three intermediate points.

To determine where your performance falls on the range, use the following table as a guide.

Excellent *4 points*	Highest expected level of results from performing this activity.
Very Good *3 points*	Fully performing this activity and has achieved original goals associated with it.
Fair *2 points*	Has most of the processes, and tools are in place, but not fully utilizing the process and/or not getting the desired results.
Poor *1 point*	People, processes, data, and/or systems are not at the minimum prescribed level, resulting in little, if any, benefit.
Not Doing *0 points*	This activity is required but currently not being performed.

This method of scoring was chosen for the following reasons: It recognizes the work people have done, even though the company may not yet be at the "Excellent" level; it indicates where, and how much, additional work is required to achieve Class A results; it provides a means for Continuous Improvement—even at the Class A level, there is still room for improvement.

Most people answer the detail questions first, then use this information as a guide for answering the overview questions.

It's important to point out that the score for the overview questions is not an average of the scores for the detail questions. The detail questions are designed to help in determining the score for the overview question, but not all questions are of equal importance.

Calculating the Letter Grade

Once the Overview Items have been answered, complete the process of determining the letter grade for the chapter by averaging the numerical scores for the Overview Items.

- Average greater than 3.5 means that you are at the Class A level for that set of business processes.
- Average between 2.5 and 3.49 qualifies for Class B level.

- Average between 1.5 and 2.49 means Class C.
- Average less than 1.5 indicates a Class D level.

Moreover, before any company can be rated with confidence, there should be *at least three months of sustained performance*. As we all know, there are periods when everything appears to be working well, but it does not necessarily mean that the company has implemented the right set of tools or has learned to manage effectively using them. A single point in time is not sufficient to arrive at a firm conclusion.

Even a Class A rating in a particular set of business processes, however, should not be interpreted as achieving full utilization of your potential. A company achieving a Class A level of performance can still get better.

For example, if the company has achieved a Class A level of excellence in New Product Development Processes, there are obviously other business functions in which Class A can be attained. In addition, achieving Class A in New Product Development Processes doesn't mean there is no room for improvement, even in that area.

Many companies take pride in attaining a Class A level and then use this accomplishment as inspiration for further improvements. In fact, all of the companies who have attained the Class A level of performance tend to be very self-critical. They continue to see what remains, what can be done, and are aggressively pushing forward.

"I know we can get a lot better and must."

"The competition is tough, but so are we."

"The emphasis in our business is to give the customer what he wants, when he wants it, with continually lower lead times and excellent quality."

These are quotes from companies that are remarkably good today, but will be even better tomorrow.

Establish Goals and Objectives

The next critically important step is to establish the goals and objectives based on the assessment. These goals lead to accountabilities for the areas that need improvement. Someone (or several people) would be assigned the accountability for meeting the goals and objectives in the planned time frame for each task in the action plan.

To prevent backsliding in areas where the assessment has shown good results, one person (or several people) would be assigned the accountability for maintaining the current level of performance on each of these items.

Tailor Checklist to Your Company's Immediate Needs

Some companies tackle a number of areas for improvement simultaneously, while others go one step at a time. It used to be the norm that companies would start with one business function, for example, quality. Once they had made significant progress in that area, they would take on another initiative, perhaps Planning and Control Processes. Today the competitive pressures are such that many companies cannot afford to implement the new competitive tools one step at a time. Many companies are implementing several different business functions at once. For example, a number of companies have initiatives in progress on Planning and Control, Total Quality, and Continuous Improvement. Taking on this much work challenges a company's ability to manage change and puts significant strain on its resources. But the results are happening, and in less time than would be required if the different business functions were improved one at a time.

The new ABCD Checklist supports the implementation of one or many initiatives. You may choose to focus your implementation on one business function or several. When this implementation work is complete, one or more additional areas would be selected for implementation. By organizing the checklist into chapters, you can select one or several chapters to include in your current implementation plans.

In addition, we have created a data base version of the checklist for personal computers. The data base capabilities of this format allow a company to tailor the checklist to its implementation activities, creating a subset of the checklist containing the items being actively worked for improvement, and focusing attention on these items. In addition, the checklist software also includes a number of powerful tailoring and project management capabilities. These would be used to record the accountabilities, milestones, and target and actual performance levels for each item.

Develop Action Plans

With the goals established, the subset of activities defined, and the accountabilities in place, each person with specific accountabilities must now develop action plans for implementation. How are the goals to be achieved, what needs to be done to improve our ability to answer this question in the future, and what are the dates for completion and improvement? These are the questions that need to be answered in this phase of the improvement process.

Measure Progress

As progress is made, it should be recorded against the action plans created. Some questions can be measured quantitatively. For example, bill of material accuracy can be plotted, showing progress from the starting point to the agreed-upon goal. Other questions are more subjective, but still capable of measurement. An example would be surveying people's perceptions on top management's commitment to quality.

Conduct Monthly Management Reviews

Experience has shown it's important to conduct monthly reviews. The purpose is to monitor progress on currently active items and watch for slippage on established items. As with any implementation management review, the questions to ask are:

- Have the milestones been achieved?
- If not, what can be done to bring this aspect of the implementation back on schedule?
- What issues need to be resolved to continue our progress?

With these steps in mind as a method for improving the operational excellence of your organization, let's now look at the five chapters of the ABCD Checklist.

1

STRATEGIC PLANNING PROCESSES

QUALITATIVE CHARACTERISTICS

Class A Strategic planning is an ongoing process and carries an intense customer focus. The strategic plan drives decisions and actions. Employees at all levels can articulate the company's mission, its vision for the future, and its overall strategic direction.

Class B A formal process, performed by line executives and managers at least once per year. Major decisions are tested first against the strategic plan. The mission and/or vision statements are widely shared.

Class C Done infrequently, but providing some direction to how the business is run.

Class D Nonexistent, or totally removed from the ongoing operation of the business.

OVERVIEW ITEMS

1-1 COMMITMENT TO EXCELLENCE
The company has an obsession with excellence; there is dissatisfaction with the status quo. Executives provide the leadership necessary for change. They articulate the motivations for positive change and other core values, and communicate them widely throughout the organization—by actions as well as by words.

1-2 BUSINESS STRATEGY/VISION
There is an explicit written business strategy that includes a vision and/or mission statement. This strategy articulates the commitment to excellence and the overriding importance of customer satisfaction.

1-3 BENCHMARKING
The company continuously measures its products, services, and practices against the toughest competitors, within and outside of the industry. This information is used to identify "best practices" and establish performance benchmarks.

1-4 SUSTAINABLE COMPETITIVE ADVANTAGE
The business strategies recognize the principle of sustainable competitive advantage: Those things not directly under the company's control may not yield competitive advantage over the long run.

1-5 ONGOING FORMAL STRATEGIC PLANNING
There is an ongoing formal strategic planning process in place, in which all senior executives have active, visible leadership roles.

1-6 CONGRUENCE TO STRATEGY

Requests for capital expenditure are tested first for congruence to the business strategy and appropriate functional strategies (i.e., does this proposal fit the strategy?).

1-7 BUSINESS PLANNING

A business planning process is used to develop and communicate annual financial plans that incorporate input from all operating departments of the company.

1-8 GENERATION OF PRODUCT COSTS

Executives and managers believe the accounting system generates valid product costs, reflecting the true costs involved in producing and delivering the company's products. Activity-based costing as well as other costing methodologies are understood, and the most suitable costing method is used.

OVERVIEW AND DETAIL ITEMS

4—EXCELLENT 3—VERY GOOD 2—FAIR 1—POOR 0—NOT DOING

1-1 COMMITMENT TO EXCELLENCE

☐ ☐ ☐ ☐ ☐

The company has an obsession with excellence; there is dissatisfaction with the status quo. Executives provide the leadership necessary for change. They articulate the motivations for positive change and other core values, and communicate them widely throughout the organization—by actions as well as by words.

1-1a   The operations functions of the business are viewed as strategically important, a source of competitive advantage on par with other functions within the business.

☐ ☐ ☐ ☐ ☐

1-1b   Commitment is demonstrated through consistent messages and via consistent decisions on resource allocations—money and people's time.

☐ ☐ ☐ ☐ ☐

1-2 BUSINESS STRATEGY/VISION

☐ ☐ ☐ ☐ ☐

There is an explicit written business strategy that includes a vision and/or mission statement. This strategy articulates the commitment to excellence and the overriding importance of customer satisfaction.

1-2a   Key people from all primary areas of the company—engineering, research and development, finance, human resources, manufacturing, marketing, sales, and others—participate deeply in the strategy development process.

☐ ☐ ☐ ☐ ☐

1-2b   The business strategy is clearly defined to provide adequate direction for all areas of the business.

☐ ☐ ☐ ☐ ☐

1-2c   The business strategy statement is widely communicated throughout the organization.

☐ ☐ ☐ ☐ ☐

1-2d   The strategic planning process addresses both internal factors (conditions the company can control) and external factors (conditions the company cannot control) that significantly affect the business.

☐ ☐ ☐ ☐ ☐

4—EXCELLENT 3—VERY GOOD 2—FAIR 1—POOR 0—NOT DOING

☐ ☐ ☐ ☐ ☐

1-3 BENCHMARKING

The company continuously measures its products, services, and practices against the toughest competitors, within and outside of the industry. This information is used to identify "best practices" and establish performance benchmarks.

1-3a   The benchmarking process is used throughout the organization to identify operational improvements and to establish effective goals and ojectives.

☐ ☐ ☐ ☐ ☐

1-3b   Benchmarks are widely communicated throughout the organization and are integrated in strategic and operating plans.

☐ ☐ ☐ ☐ ☐

1-3c   Benchmarks are periodically reviewed and recalibrated to ensure that latest developments in "best practices" and performance achievements are recognized.

☐ ☐ ☐ ☐ ☐

1-4 SUSTAINABLE COMPETITIVE ADVANTAGE

The business strategies recognize the principle of sustainable competitive advantage: Those things not directly under the company's control may not yield competitive advantage over the long run.

☐ ☐ ☐ ☐ ☐

1-4a   The company's strategies encourage the in-house development of strategically important competencies and technologies.

☐ ☐ ☐ ☐ ☐

4—EXCELLENT
3—VERY GOOD
2—FAIR
1—POOR
0—NOT DOI

1-4b In its decisions on vertical integration, ☐ ☐ ☐ ☐ ☐
make-or-buy, and equipment acquisition,
the company is guided heavily by the principle of sustainable competitive advantage.

1-5 ONGOING FORMAL STRATEGIC   ☐ ☐ ☐ ☐ ☐
PLANNING
*There is an ongoing formal strategic planning
process in place, in which all senior executives
have active, visible leadership roles.*

1-5a The business strategies are reviewed at ☐ ☐ ☐ ☐ ☐
least annually (more frequently in periods
of high change) to ensure continuing validity and congruence with one another.

1-5b Senior management, as a group, reviews ☐ ☐ ☐ ☐ ☐
progress on all major development and improvement initiatives at least once per
quarter.

1-5c The strategy statements are used by the ☐ ☐ ☐ ☐ ☐
appropriate people as a guide in develop-
ing the business plan as well as the sales
and operations plans.

1-6 CONGRUENCE TO STRATEGY   ☐ ☐ ☐ ☐ ☐
*Requests for capital expenditure are tested first
for congruence to the business strategy and
appropriate functional strategies (i.e., does this
proposal fit the strategy?).*

4—EXCELLENT 3—VERY GOOD 2—FAIR 1—POOR 0—NOT DOING

1-6a   People throughout the organization are encouraged to identify and promote all improvement opportunities, including those requiring capital expenditures.

☐ ☐ ☐ ☐ ☐

1-6b   Care is taken to ensure that return-on-investment criteria and other financial requirements do not inhibit strategically valid projects from being considered.

☐ ☐ ☐ ☐ ☐

1-6c   Payback on capital investments is measured not only via financial means but also via the impact on customer satisfaction, quality, flexibility, and delivery.

☐ ☐ ☐ ☐ ☐

1-7 BUSINESS PLANNING

☐ ☐ ☐ ☐ ☐

A business planning process is used to develop and communicate annual financial plans that incorporate input from all operating departments of the company.

1-7a   The strategic plans drive the business planning process: All annual financial plans are congruent with the business strategies.

☐ ☐ ☐ ☐ ☐

1-7b   The business plan provides specific direction regarding market share, financial performance, new product development, customer service levels, and desired inventory levels to be used in the sales and operations planning (S&OP) process.

☐ ☐ ☐ ☐ ☐

4—EXCELLENT 3—VERY GOOD 2—FAIR 1—POOR 0—NOT DONE

1-7c   The business plan horizon is long enough to support the company's sales and operations planning process.

☐ ☐ ☐ ☐ ☐

1-7d   The business plan is developed at least annually and reviewed at least quarterly (more frequently if business conditions change significantly).

☐ ☐ ☐ ☐ ☐

1-7e   The underlying assumptions used to develop the business plan are adequately documented.

☐ ☐ ☐ ☐ ☐

1-7f   A mechanism is in place to check that the sales and operations plan is synchronized with the business plan.

☐ ☐ ☐ ☐ ☐

1-7g   The business plan provides a detailed financial plan by department. All senior management people, and others as appropriate, participate in development of the business plan. Department managers review progress against the business plan on a monthly basis.

☐ ☐ ☐ ☐ ☐

1-7h   The financial projections developed in the sales and operations planning process are linked to the company's financial plans. When the S&OP financial projections differ from the business plan, the differences are reconciled and either the sales and operations plan and/or the business plan is updated.

☐ ☐ ☐ ☐ ☐

4—EXCELLENT
3—VERY GOOD
2—FAIR
1—POOR
0—NOT DOING

□ □ □ □ □

1-8 GENERATION OF PRODUCT COSTS

Executives and managers believe the accounting system generates valid product costs, reflecting the true costs involved in producing and delivering the company's products. Activity-based costing as well as other costing methodologies are understood, and the most suitable costing method is used.

1-8a   The cost system clearly distinguishes between value-adding and nonvalue-adding cost.

□ □ □ □ □

1-8b   There is a program in place to reduce or eliminate nonvalue-adding cost.

□ □ □ □ □

1-8c   Management recognizes what portion of its cost is direct labor, material, and overhead. Its focus and systems support the major cost category.

□ □ □ □ □

1-8d   The cost system can adequately support product costing, pricing, investments, make-or-buy decisions, and cost-reduction activities.

□ □ □ □ □

2

PEOPLE/TEAM PROCESSES

QUALITATIVE CHARACTERISTICS

Class A Trust, teamwork, mutual respect, open communications, and a high degree of employment security are hallmarks of the employee/company relationship. Employees are very pleased with the company and proud to be a part of it.

Class B Employees have confidence in the company's management and consider the company a good place to work. Effective use being made of small work groups.

Class C Traditional employment practices are largely being used. Management considers the company's people to be an important, but not vital, resource of the business.

Class D The employee/employer relationship is neutral at best, sometimes negative.

OVERVIEW ITEMS

2-1 COMMITMENT TO EXCELLENCE

All levels of management have a commitment to treating people with trust, openness, and honesty. Teams are used to multiply the strength of the organization. People are empowered to take direct action, make decisions, and initiate changes.

2-2 CULTURE

A comprehensive culture exists to support and enhance effective people and team processes.

2-3 TRUST

Openness, honesty, and constructive feedback are highly valued and demonstrated organizational traits.

2-4 TEAMWORK†

Clearly identifiable teams are utilized as the primary means to organize the work, as opposed to individual job functions or independent work stations.

2-5 EMPLOYMENT CONTINUITY†

Employment continuity is an important company goal as long as the employee exceeds the minimum acceptable job requirements and the level of business is viable.

2-6 EDUCATION AND TRAINING†

An active education and training process for all employees is in place focused on business and customer issues and improvements. Its objectives include Continuous Improvement, enhancing the empowered worker, flexibility, employment stability, and meeting future needs.

2-7 WORK DESIGN†
Jobs are designed to reinforce the company goal of a team-based, empowered work force.

2-8 CONGRUENCE
People policies, organizational development, and education and training maintain consistency with the company vision and business strategies.

OVERVIEW AND DETAIL ITEMS

2-1 COMMITMENT TO EXCELLENCE*

All levels of management have a commitment to treating people with trust, openness, and honesty. Teams are used to multiply the strength of the organization. People are empowered to take direct action, make decisions, and initiate changes.

4—EXCELLENT 3—VERY GOOD 2—FAIR 1—POOR 0—NOT DOING

☐ ☐ ☐ ☐ ☐

2-2 CULTURE

A comprehensive culture exists to support and enhance effective people and team processes.

☐ ☐ ☐ ☐ ☐

2-2a   Operators are empowered to take direct action whenever they encounter a problem that is likely to impact quality, cost, schedule, and/or input.

☐ ☐ ☐ ☐ ☐

2-2b   There are few "status" distinctions between managers and workers. There is a clear intention to minimize artificial barriers that would be detrimental to creating an open, highly empowered work environment.

☐ ☐ ☐ ☐ ☐

2-2c   Information-passing processes such as team meetings and regular "state-of-the-business" assemblies are a regular part of work.

□ □ □ □ □

2-2d   A process is in place to help workers expand their role to become team players, highly skilled, knowledge resources, customer advocates, trainers, problem solvers, and decision makers. This process includes training and follow-up support.

□ □ □ □ □

2-2e   A process is in place to help supervisors, managers, and technical and support professionals modify and expand their roles to become coaches, facilitators, customer advocates, barrier busters, motivators, and leaders. This process includes training and follow-up support.

□ □ □ □ □

2-2f   Major achievements stemming from the Continuous Improvement and empowerment efforts are formally celebrated.

□ □ □ □ □

2-2g   The important lessons learned from the empowerment and change efforts have been formally documented and are being integrated into future organization development plans.

□ □ □ □ □

4—EXCELLENT 3—VERY GOOD 2—FAIR 1—POOR 0—NOT DOING

☐ ☐ ☐ ☐ ☐

2-3 TRUST

Openness, honesty, and constructive feedback are highly valued and demonstrated organizational traits.

2-3a Continuously improving communications between management and workers is stated as an important company objective and is occurring.

☐ ☐ ☐ ☐ ☐

2-3b The information flow is adequate and timely enough for people at all levels to understand the current performance of the business (e.g., customers, competition, strategies, profitability) and effectively utilize operational data (e.g., quality, service level, schedule, etc.) for problem identification, resolution, and improvement recommendations.

☐ ☐ ☐ ☐ ☐

2-3c Management regularly provides customer/ supplier feedback and sets up opportunities for direct, face-to-face meetings between team members and customers/ suppliers. These communication linkages are regularly used to identify process and product improvements.

☐ ☐ ☐ ☐ ☐

2-3d Manager and peer feedback occur on a routine basis. Managers also receive regular feedback from the people they manage.

☐ ☐ ☐ ☐ ☐

2-3e A performance-measurement system has been put in place or modified to provide ongoing feedback to teams and individuals.

☐ ☐ ☐ ☐ ☐

4—EXCELLENT
3—VERY GOOD
2—FAIR
1—POOR
0—NOT DONE

☐ ☐ ☐ ☐ ☐

2-4 TEAMWORK†
*Clearly identifiable teams are utilized as the
primary means to organize the work, as opposed
to individual job functions or independent work
stations.*

2-4a   All team members, managers, super-   ☐ ☐ ☐ ☐ ☐
visors, and technical and support people
have been formally introduced to the concepts of high-performance work teams
through educational experience.

2-4b   The roles/jobs have been formally struc-   ☐ ☐ ☐ ☐ ☐
tured to support the work team approach.

2-4c   Each team has developed a clearly defined   ☐ ☐ ☐ ☐ ☐
charter/mission and operating guidelines.

2-4d   Each team meets regularly and frequently   ☐ ☐ ☐ ☐ ☐
to solve problems and explore oppor-
tunities in its work area.

2-4e   The work teams and the functions they   ☐ ☐ ☐ ☐ ☐
perform are almost entirely self-contained
and managed by the group itself. Group
members rely on one another for cross
training, problem solving, the handling of
administrative duties, and mutual support.

2-4f   A structured method to examine the work   ☐ ☐ ☐ ☐ ☐
flow and processes is conducted by work
teams to improve the effectiveness of the
operation.

2-4g   Each work group has a defined process for gaining direct feedback from both external and internal customers.

☐ ☐ ☐ ☐ ☐

2-4h   The requirements of customers, external and internal, are visible in the work area.

☐ ☐ ☐ ☐ ☐

2-4i   Work teams are directly involved in establishing quantitative and qualitative measurements to track the operational effectiveness of the group. This information provides feedback to the teams relating to their overall performance.

☐ ☐ ☐ ☐ ☐

2-5 EMPLOYMENT CONTINUITY†

☐ ☐ ☐ ☐ ☐

Employment continuity is an important company goal as long as the employee exceeds the minimum acceptable job requirements and the level of business is viable.

2-5a   The goal of employment continuity is clearly articulated and widely communicated throughout the organization.

☐ ☐ ☐ ☐ ☐

2-5b   Effective employment planning is in place to help reduce the negative effects of rapid change in demand and/or growth and achieve the goal of employment continuity.

☐ ☐ ☐ ☐ ☐

4—EXCELLENT 3—VERY GOOD 2—FAIR 1—POOR 0—NOT DOING

□ □ □ □ □

2-6 EDUCATION AND TRAINING†

An active education and training process for all employees is in place focused on business and customer issues and improvements. Its objectives include Continuous Improvement, enhancing the empowered worker, flexibility, employment stability, and meeting future needs.

2-6a   Management attitude and actions demonstrate a commitment to fully educate and train people prior to implementation of new technologies and processes.

□ □ □ □ □

2-6b   Education is a participative process rather than a one-directional flow from the top of the organization to the bottom.

□ □ □ □ □

2-6c   The education and training process recognizes people at all levels as experts in their areas, communicates objectives, and fully involves people in the process of changing their jobs.

□ □ □ □ □

2-6d   The education and training approach is based on the principles of behavior change in an organization rather than merely a process of fact transfer regarding a specific technology.

□ □ □ □ □

2-6e   The company has committed sufficient resources, financial and otherwise, to education and training.

□ □ □ □ □

4—EXCELLENT
3—VERY GOOD
2—FAIR
1—POOR
0—NOT DOING

2-6f   An ongoing education and training process is used to refine and improve the use of business tools like team-based technologies, Just-in-Time (JIT), Total Quality Control (TQC), Manufacturing Resource Planning system (MRP II), etc.   ☐ ☐ ☐ ☐ ☐

2-6g   Areas of employee improvement needs are continuously assessed.   ☐ ☐ ☐ ☐ ☐

2-7 WORK DESIGN†   ☐ ☐ ☐ ☐ ☐
Jobs are designed to reinforce the company goal of a team-based, empowered work force.

2-7a   Skill training is formalized and managed to create the desired level of flexibility.   ☐ ☐ ☐ ☐ ☐

2-7b   A performance management system is in place to provide ongoing feedback to teams and individuals.   ☐ ☐ ☐ ☐ ☐

2-7c   A compensation strategy exists that recognizes, rewards, and reinforces behaviors and results that support the business strategy.   ☐ ☐ ☐ ☐ ☐

2-8 CONGRUENCE   ☐ ☐ ☐ ☐ ☐
People policies, organizational development, and education and training maintain consistency with the company vision and business strategies.

4—EXCELLENT 3—VERY GOOD 2—FAIR 1—POOR 0—NOT DONE

2-8a   Everyone in the organization can state who the key customers, key competitors, and key suppliers are. They can also describe what differentiates the product/service they build/support from others in the marketplace.

2-8b   The performance management factors for teams and individuals are reviewed and updated to reflect changes in the business objectives and the work process.

2-8c   Employee satisfaction measures are taken and monitored regularly, such as attitude surveys, absenteeism, and turnover. Baseline numbers have been established and positive trends are evident.

3

TOTAL QUALITY AND CONTINUOUS IMPROVEMENT PROCESSES

QUALITATIVE CHARACTERISTICS

Class A Continuous improvement has become a way of life for employees, suppliers, and customers. Improved quality, reduced costs, and increased velocity are contributing to a competitive advantage. There is a targeted strategy for innovation.

Class B Most departments are participating in these processes; they have active involvement with suppliers and customers. Substantial improvements have been made in many areas.

Class C Processes are being utilized in limited areas; some departmental improvements have been achieved.

Class D Processes not established, or processes established but static.

OVERVIEW ITEMS

3-1 COMMITMENT TO EXCELLENCE

There is a commitment to total quality in all areas of the business and to continuous improvements in customer satisfaction, employee development, delivery, and cost.

3-2 TOP MANAGEMENT LEADERSHIP FOR QUALITY AND CONTINUOUS IMPROVEMENT

Top executives are actively involved in establishing and communicating the organization's vision, goals, plans, and values for quality and Continuous Improvement.

3-3 FOCUS ON CUSTOMER

A variety of effective techniques is used to ensure that customer needs are identified, prioritized, and satisfied. Customers are identified both internally and externally, and all functions participate. External customers include users, other external links in the chain to the end user, shareholders, stakeholders, and community.

3-4 CUSTOMER PARTNERSHIPS

Strong "partnership" relationships that are mutually beneficial are being established with customers.

3-5 CONTINUOUS ELIMINATION OF WASTE

There is a company-wide commitment to the continuous and relentless elimination of waste. A formal program is used to expose, prioritize, and stimulate the elimination of nonvalue-adding activities.

3-6 ROUTINE USE OF TOTAL QUALITY CONTROL TOOLS

Routine use of the basic tools of Total Quality Control and the practice of mistake proofing has become a way of life in virtually all areas of the company.

3-7 RESOURCES AND FACILITIES—FLEXIBILITY, COST, QUALITY

Resources and facilities required to economically receive, produce, and ship the product are continuously being made more flexible, cost effective, and capable of producing higher quality.

3-8 PRODUCE TO CUSTOMER ORDERS

The time required to manufacture products has been reduced such that the planning and control system uses forecasts to project material and capacity needs, but production of finished products is based on actual customer orders or distribution demands (except where strategic or seasonal inventories are being built).

3-9 SUPPLIER PARTNERSHIPS

Strong "partnership" relationships that are mutually beneficial are being established with fewer but better suppliers, to facilitate improvements in quality, cost, and overall responsiveness.

3-10 PROCUREMENT—QUALITY, RESPONSIVENESS, COST

The procurement process is continuously being improved and simplified to improve quality and responsiveness while simultaneously reducing the total procurement costs.

3-11 KANBAN

Kanban is being effectively used to control production where its use will provide significant benefit.

3-12 VELOCITY

The velocity and linearity of flow is continuously being measured and improved.

3-13 ACCOUNTING SIMPLIFICATION

Accounting procedures and paperwork are being simplified, eliminating nonvalue-adding activities, while at the same time providing the ability to generate product costs sufficiently accurate to use in decision making and satisfy audit requirements.

3-14 USE OF TOTAL QUALITY CONTROL AND JUST-IN-TIME

A minimum of 80 percent of the plant output is produced using the tools and techniques of TQC and JIT.

3-15 TEAMWORK†

Clearly identifiable teams are utilized as the primary means to organize the work, as opposed to individual job functions or independent work stations.

3-16 EDUCATION AND TRAINING†

An active education and training process for all employees is in place focused on business and customer issues and improvement. Its objectives include Continuous Improvement, enhancing the empowered worker, flexibility, employment stability, and meeting future needs.

3-17 WORK DESIGN†

Jobs are designed to reinforce the company goal of a team-based, empowered work force.

3-18 EMPLOYMENT CONTINUITY†

Employment continuity is an important company goal as long as the employee exceeds the minimum acceptable job requirements and the level of business is viable.

3-19 COMPANY PERFORMANCE—QUALITY, DELIVERY, COST

Company performance measurements emphasize quality, delivery, and cost. Performance measures are communicated to all through visible displays that show progress and point the way to improvement (e.g., run charts coupled with Pareto charts).

3-20 SETTING AND ATTAINING QUALITY GOALS

Short- and long-term quality goals that cause the organization to stretch are established, regularly reviewed, and monitored. These goals are targeted on improvements in total cost, cycle time (or response time), and customer quality requirements.

OVERVIEW AND DETAIL ITEMS

4—EXCELLENT
3—VERY GOOD
2—FAIR
1—POOR
0—NOT DONE

3-1 COMMITMENT TO EXCELLENCE*
□ □ □ □ □

There is a commitment to total quality in all areas of the business and to continuous improvements in customer satisfaction, employee development, delivery, and cost.

3-2 TOP MANAGEMENT LEADERSHIP FOR QUALITY AND CONTINUOUS IMPROVEMENT
□ □ □ □ □

Top executives are actively involved in establishing and communicating the organization's vision, goals, plans, and values for quality and Continuous Improvement.

3-2a   A belief in Continuous Improvement is exhibited through strategies and actions at all levels of management.
□ □ □ □ □

3-2b   Resources such as time, training, and money are provided throughout the organization oriented toward the improvement of quality and innovation.
□ □ □ □ □

3-2c   The environment encourages innovation, pride of work, open horizontal and vertical communication, information and resource sharing, and cross-department cooperation.
□ □ □ □ □

3-2d   All employees are encouraged to contribute to improvements in processes and systems.
□ □ □ □ □

4—EXCELLENT 3—VERY GOOD 2—FAIR 1—POOR 0—NOT DOING

3-2e   Management routinely removes barriers to performance, innovation, and quality.

☐ ☐ ☐ ☐ ☐

3-2f   The extent to which quality values, principles, and practices are adopted is routinely reviewed and improved.

☐ ☐ ☐ ☐ ☐

3-2g   Top management is in routine contact with customers, suppliers, and employees.

☐ ☐ ☐ ☐ ☐

3-3 FOCUS ON CUSTOMER

☐ ☐ ☐ ☐ ☐

A variety of effective techniques is used to ensure that customer needs are identified, prioritized, and satisfied. Customers are identified both internally and externally, and all functions participate. External customers include users, other external links in the chain to the end user, shareholders, stakeholders, and community.

3-3a   Mechanisms for establishing and prioritizing customer needs and requirements exist and are regularly used. Features and rankings indicating relative importance are clearly identified for products and services.

☐ ☐ ☐ ☐ ☐

3-3b   Processes are in place that ensure customer feedback and complaint-driven improvements get corrective action and appropriate priority.

☐ ☐ ☐ ☐ ☐

4—EXCELLENT 3—VERY GOOD 2—FAIR 1—POOR 0—NOT DOING

3-3c   Management actively seeks ways to ensure that all employees are aware of customer needs and expectations. Mechanisms are in place, and constantly improving, to understand and fulfill these needs.

3-3d   Easy access by customers to information and problem resolution is assured and measured.

3-3e   Service goals to exceed customer expectations are tracked, reported, and used for improvement planning and implementation.

3-3f   Customer-feedback systems are evaluated and improved. Changing customer patterns are monitored and evaluated as part of this process.

3-3g   Customer-contact employees have sufficient authority and empowerment to resolve customer problems.

3-4 CUSTOMER PARTNERSHIPS
Strong "partnership" relationships that are mutually beneficial are being established with customers.

3-4a   Marketing and sales view Just-in-Time/ Total Quality Control as a competitive weapon in the marketplace.

3-4b   Long-term, mutually beneficial relation-   ☐ ☐ ☐ ☐ ☐
ships with customers are being pursued to
facilitate improvements in quality, cost,
and overall customer satisfaction.

3-4c   Direct communications have been estab-   ☐ ☐ ☐ ☐ ☐
lished to improve responsiveness between
the company's operating departments and
the customers' operating departments.

3-4d   Lead time from receipt of customer order   ☐ ☐ ☐ ☐ ☐
at the company to receipt of the product by
the customer is continuously being reduced.

3-4e   Continuous Improvement is being encour-   ☐ ☐ ☐ ☐ ☐
aged, where applicable, throughout the
customer base.

3-4f   Transportation costs to distribution centers   ☐ ☐ ☐ ☐ ☐
and to customers are being reduced while
delivery frequency is increasing.

3-4g   Kanbans are being used with customers,   ☐ ☐ ☐ ☐ ☐
where applicable.

3-5 CONTINUOUS ELIMINATION OF   ☐ ☐ ☐ ☐ ☐
WASTE
There is a company-wide commitment to the
continuous and relentless elimination of waste. A
formal program is used to expose, prioritize, and
stimulate the elimination of nonvalue-adding
activities.

4—EXCELLENT
3— VERY GOOD
2—FAIR
1—POOR
0—NOT DOIN

3-5a   A formal, visible, and continuous process to improve responsiveness is in place (reducing and eliminating lead times, order quantities, safety stocks, queues, and all other nonvalue-adding activities). All employees can articulate the essence of this process.   ☐ ☐ ☐ ☐ ☐

3-5b   The number of kanbans is being continuously reduced to expose, prioritize, and stimulate problem solving.   ☐ ☐ ☐ ☐ ☐

3-5c   Lot sizes or batch sizes are continually being reduced.   ☐ ☐ ☐ ☐ ☐

3-5d   All lead times are being systematically and continuously reduced.   ☐ ☐ ☐ ☐ ☐

3-5e   The number of item numbers is being reduced through standardization.   ☐ ☐ ☐ ☐ ☐

3-5f   An ongoing effort to increase the reliability of on-time completions and to decrease lead times within the product development functions is highly visible and generating improvements.   ☐ ☐ ☐ ☐ ☐

3-5g   Engineering changes are analyzed using Total Quality Control methods to reduce their number and associated costs.   ☐ ☐ ☐ ☐ ☐

3-5h   The need for separate inspection activities is being eliminated or reduced.   ☐ ☐ ☐ ☐ ☐

3-5i   A formal and active program exists to reduce scrap, shrinkage, and rework, and to increase yields.   ☐ ☐ ☐ ☐ ☐

4—EXCELLENT 3—VERY GOOD 2—FAIR 1—POOR 0—NOT DOING

3-5j Employees at all levels and in all areas are contributing ideas for, and participating in, waste elimination.

□ □ □ □ □

3-6 ROUTINE USE OF TOTAL QUALITY CONTROL TOOLS

□ □ □ □ □

Routine use of the basic tools of Total Quality Control and the practice of mistake proofing has become a way of life in virtually all areas of the company.

3-6a Each functional area has established a set of key internal and/or external customer-satisfaction measures, tracks performance, and seeks the root cause of variations.

□ □ □ □ □

3-6b The use of data acts as a common language among all employees in all functional areas when dealing with quality problems.

□ □ □ □ □

3-6c Cause-and-effect diagrams are used routinely throughout the organization.

□ □ □ □ □

3-6d Key problems under attack are shown in visible displays containing information about the team members, root cause and variation analysis, actions, and results.

□ □ □ □ □

3-6e Control charts are used where appropriate, but are not the only TQC tool in evidence.

□ □ □ □ □

3-6f Flow charts are used to document key processes in manufacturing and other areas.

□ □ □ □ □

4—EXCELLENT
3—VERY GOOD
2—FAIR
1—POOR
0—NOT DOING

3-6g   Where more than one way to do something exists, consideration is routinely given to eliminating the variation by mistake proofing the activity. This has become a common practice in all areas of the company.

3-6h   Multiple levels of Pareto charts are used to identify the root cause, where appropriate.

3-6i   Inspection, in all areas, is viewed as waste. Inspection is viewed as a way to purchase information. Inspection, in the future, will be reduced as that information is used to prevent variation in the product or process.

3-7 RESOURCES AND FACILITIES— FLEXIBILITY, COST, QUALITY

Resources and facilities required to economically receive, produce, and ship the product are continuously being made more flexible, cost effective, and capable of producing higher quality.

3-7a   Plant and office layouts are being continually improved to simplify and reduce the physical transport of material (e.g., distance and handling minimized, communications and visibility maximized).

3-7b   Equipment is selected based on its contribution to improved quality, fast setups, minimum lot sizes, flexibility, and overall throughput time. A policy exists to justify equipment based on these factors in addition to traditional selection criteria.

4—EXCELLENT 3—VERY GOOD 2—FAIR 1—POOR 0—NOT DOING

3-7c   Authorization for capital spending places high value on the company's drive to improve quality and increase the velocity of the material flow from suppliers through the plant and out to the customer.   ☐ ☐ ☐ ☐ ☐

3-7d   Simplified manufacturing processes with visual controls are in place, allowing problems to be quickly identified.   ☐ ☐ ☐ ☐ ☐

3-7e   Tools and fixtures are stored primarily at the point of use.   ☐ ☐ ☐ ☐ ☐

3-7f   Setup and changeover times are being systematically and continuously reduced thereby enabling manufacturing lot sizes to be economically reduced.   ☐ ☐ ☐ ☐ ☐

3-7g   A preventive-maintenance program is in place for equipment and tooling.   ☐ ☐ ☐ ☐ ☐

3-7h   Unplanned machine downtime is documented and being reduced.   ☐ ☐ ☐ ☐ ☐

3-7i   Where appropriate, materials are stored primarily at the point of use and/or at the point of manufacture rather than in a central stockroom.   ☐ ☐ ☐ ☐ ☐

3-7j   Good housekeeping (orderliness) is being pursued as a high-priority item by all personnel.   ☐ ☐ ☐ ☐ ☐

4—EXCELLENT 3—VERY GOOD 2—FAIR 1—POOR 0—NOT DO

☐ ☐ ☐ ☐ ☐

3-8 PRODUCE TO CUSTOMER ORDERS

The time required to manufacture products has been reduced such that the planning and control system uses forecasts to project material and capacity needs, but production of finished products is based on actual customer orders or distribution demands (except where strategic or seasonal inventories are being built).

3-8a   Formal planning systems (such as MRP II) are used for internal resources planning, customer commitments, and supplier capacity planning.

☐ ☐ ☐ ☐ ☐

3-8b   Mixed-model scheduling from master scheduling through the entire manufacturing process into purchasing is utilized widely.

☐ ☐ ☐ ☐ ☐

3-8c   The physical movement of materials within the factory is triggered by consumption (e.g., a kanban signal).

☐ ☐ ☐ ☐ ☐

3-8d   Daily, or shorter, production rates are being emphasized rather than large batches.

☐ ☐ ☐ ☐ ☐

3-8e   Information is available to operations people in a timely manner, and a concurrent goal exists to simplify and reduce or eliminate the number of transactions and reports.

☐ ☐ ☐ ☐ ☐

Rating scale: 4—EXCELLENT 3—VERY GOOD 2—FAIR 1—POOR 0—NOT DOING

3-9 SUPPLIER PARTNERSHIPS

Strong "partnership" relationships that are mutually beneficial are being established with fewer but better suppliers, to facilitate improvements in quality, cost, and overall responsiveness.

3-9a   The number of suppliers is being reduced, and single sourcing, where practical, is a stated company objective.

3-9b   Just-in-Time/Total Quality Control are being encouraged throughout the supplier base.

3-9c   Supplier selection is based more on the total cost of acquisition rather than on the lowest purchase price.

3-9d   Long-term contracts (e.g., multiyear, life of product) are being established with the key suppliers who supply 80 percent of the purchased volume.

3-9e   Purchasing by kanban authorization, based on contractual agreement, is being aggressively pursued with an increasing number of suppliers. A significant percentage of the purchased volume is already under kanban authorization.

3-9f   Key suppliers participate in the development and design of new products.

4—EXCELLENT 3—VERY GOOD 2—FAIR 1—POOR 0—NOT DOING

□ □ □ □ □

3-10 PROCUREMENT—QUALITY, RESPONSIVENESS, COST

The procurement process is continuously being improved and simplified to improve quality and responsiveness while simultaneously reducing the total procurement costs.

3-10a   Projections of future requirements for purchased items are shared with suppliers to ensure adequate capacity to support business requirements. These future projections extend out beyond the suppliers quoted lead times.

□ □ □ □ □

3-10b   Suppliers are provided with output reports (e.g., supplier schedules) from the formal planning system.

□ □ □ □ □

3-10c   Purchase order releases have been reduced or eliminated and replaced by kanban signals for an increasing percentage of the purchased volume.

□ □ □ □ □

3-10d   Suppliers are being certified to reduce/ eliminate source inspection, receiving inspection, and count verification.

□ □ □ □ □

3-10e   Delivery quantities are being economically reduced, resulting in more frequent deliveries of smaller quantities from suppliers.

□ □ □ □ □

3-10f   Transportation costs from suppliers are being decreased even though delivery frequency is being increased.

□ □ □ □ □

4—EXCELLENT 3—VERY GOOD 2—FAIR 1—POOR 0—NOT DOING

3-10g Materials go directly from dock to point of use rather than from dock to stock. Central stockrooms are viewed primarily as overflow locations.

☐ ☐ ☐ ☐ ☐

3-10h A supplier rating system has been developed and implemented, and is being used to trigger improvements in supplier performance.

☐ ☐ ☐ ☐ ☐

3-10i Suppliers practice value analysis/value engineering techniques and make recommendations to improve quality, cost, and responsiveness for both current and new products.

☐ ☐ ☐ ☐ ☐

3-10j Direct communications have been established to improve responsiveness between the company's operating departments and the suppliers' operating departments.

☐ ☐ ☐ ☐ ☐

3-11 KANBAN

☐ ☐ ☐ ☐ ☐

Kanban is being effectively used to control production where its use will provide significant benefit.

3-11a Material is not moved to a work station that does not have an open kanban.

☐ ☐ ☐ ☐ ☐

3-11b Work is not started at a work station that does not have an open kanban.

☐ ☐ ☐ ☐ ☐

4—EXCELLENT
3—VERY GOOD
2—FAIR
1—POOR
0—NOT DOING

3-11c   The principle of quality at the source is understood and has resulted in employees being empowered to stop production rather than pass on a known defect.

☐ ☐ ☐ ☐ ☐

3-11d   There has been no more than one kanban violation during the last ninety days.

☐ ☐ ☐ ☐ ☐

3-11e   There have been no more than six approved kanban limit exceptions during the last twelve months.

☐ ☐ ☐ ☐ ☐

3-12 VELOCITY

The velocity and linearity of flow is continuously being measured and improved.

☐ ☐ ☐ ☐ ☐

3-12a   Functional work centers are being replaced by cells, where appropriate.

☐ ☐ ☐ ☐ ☐

3-12b   Production lines are being designed to enable mixed-model production with minimum material handling.

☐ ☐ ☐ ☐ ☐

3-12c   Process improvements are being made such that routings are being simplified.

☐ ☐ ☐ ☐ ☐

3-12d   Bills of material are being flattened (or phantom codes are being used) to improve velocity.

☐ ☐ ☐ ☐ ☐

3-12e   Nonmanufacturing processes such as order entry, product development, accounts receivable, etc. are being simplified to improve velocity in these areas.

☐ ☐ ☐ ☐ ☐

4—EXCELLENT 3—VERY GOOD 2—FAIR 1—POOR 0—NOT DOING

3-13 ACCOUNTING SIMPLIFICATION
☐ ☐ ☐ ☐ ☐

Accounting procedures and paperwork are being simplified, eliminating nonvalue-adding activities, while at the same time providing the ability to generate product costs sufficiently accurate to use in decision making and satisfy audit requirements.

3-13a Work orders are either being eliminated or reduced and no longer used for detail tracking of labor and material.
☐ ☐ ☐ ☐ ☐

3-13b Labor collection procedures are being simplified (e.g., groupings of direct and indirect labor operations, labor collection by exception, etc.).
☐ ☐ ☐ ☐ ☐

3-13c Activity-based costing is clearly understood by people in top management, finance, and manufacturing; it is being used in situations where it can provide significant benefit to the business.
☐ ☐ ☐ ☐ ☐

3-14 USE OF TOTAL QUALITY CONTROL AND JUST-IN-TIME*
☐ ☐ ☐ ☐ ☐

A minimum of 80 percent of the plant output is produced using the tools and techniques of TQC and JIT.

4—EXCELLENT
3—VERY GOOD
2—FAIR
1—POOR
0—NOT DOIN

3-15 TEAMWORK†

Clearly identifiable teams are utilized as the primary means to organize the work, as opposed to individual job functions or independent work stations.

3-15a   All team members, managers, supervisors, and technical and support people have been formally introduced to the concepts of high-performance work teams through educational experience.

3-15b   The roles/jobs have been formally structured to support the work team approach.

3-15c   Each team has developed a clearly defined charter/mission and operating guidelines.

3-15d   Each team meets regularly and frequently to solve problems and explore opportunities in its work area.

3-15e   The work teams and the functions they perform are almost entirely self-contained and managed by the group itself. Group members rely on one another for cross training, problem solving, the handling of administrative duties, and mutual support.

3-15f   A structured method to examine the work flow and processes is conducted by work teams to improve the effectiveness of the operation.

4—EXCELLENT 3—VERY GOOD 2—FAIR 1—POOR 0—NOT DOING

3-15g Each work group has a defined process for gaining direct feedback from both external and internal customers.

☐ ☐ ☐ ☐ ☐

3-15h The requirements of customers, external and internal, are visible in the work area.

☐ ☐ ☐ ☐ ☐

3-15i Work teams are directly involved in establishing quantitative and qualitative measurements to track the operational effectiveness of the group. This information provides feedback to the teams relating to their overall performance.

☐ ☐ ☐ ☐ ☐

3-15j Quality problems and other opportunities for waste elimination are addressed by a team of the most appropriate people regardless of their reporting level in the organization.

☐ ☐ ☐ ☐ ☐

3-16 EDUCATION AND TRAINING†

An active education and training process for all employees is in place focused on business and customer issues and improvements. Its objectives include Continuous Improvement, enhancing the empowered worker, flexibility, employment stability, and meeting future needs.

☐ ☐ ☐ ☐ ☐

3-16a Management attitude and actions demonstrate a commitment to fully educate and train people prior to implementation of new technologies and processes.

☐ ☐ ☐ ☐ ☐

4—EXCELLENT
3—VERY GOOD
2—FAIR
1—POOR
0—NOT DOING

3-16b   Education is a participative process rather than a one-directional flow from the top of the organization to the bottom.

3-16c   The education and training process recognizes people at all levels as experts in their areas, communicates objectives, and fully involves people in the process of changing their jobs.

3-16d   The education and training approach is based on the principles of behavior change in an organization rather than merely a process of fact transfer regarding a specific technology.

3-16e   The company has committed sufficient resources, financial and otherwise, to education and training.

3-16f   An ongoing education and training process is used to refine and improve the use of business tools like team-based technologies, Just-in-Time (JIT), Total Quality Control (TQC), Manufacturing Resource Planning system (MRP II), etc.

3-16g   Areas of employee improvement needs are continuously assessed.

3-17 WORK DESIGN†
Jobs are designed to reinforce the company goal of a team-based, empowered work force.

3-17a   Skill training is formalized and managed to create the desired level of flexibility.

4—EXCELLENT 3—VERY GOOD 2—FAIR 1—POOR 0—NOT DOING

3-17b A performance management system is in place to provide ongoing feedback to teams and individuals. ☐☐☐☐☐

3-17c A compensation strategy exists that recognizes, rewards, and reinforces those behaviors and results that support the business strategy. ☐☐☐☐☐

3-18 EMPLOYMENT CONTINUITY† ☐☐☐☐☐

Employment continuity is an important company goal as long as the employee exceeds the minimum acceptable job requirements and the level of business is viable.

3-18a The goal of employment continuity is clearly articulated and widely communicated throughout the organization. ☐☐☐☐☐

3-18b Effective employment planning is in place to help reduce the negative effects of rapid change in demand and/or growth and achieve the goal of employment continuity. ☐☐☐☐☐

3-19 COMPANY PERFORMANCE—QUALITY, DELIVERY, COST ☐☐☐☐☐

Company performance measurements emphasize quality, delivery, and cost. Performance measures are communicated to all through visible displays that show progress and point the way to improvement (e.g., run charts coupled with Pareto charts).

4—EXCELLENT 3—VERY GOOD 2—FAIR 1—POOR 0—NOT DO

3-19a   Valid, timely information is collected and analyzed on all products and services for external customers and significant and targeted internal customers and suppliers.   □ □ □ □ □

3-19b   A data-and-information collection process exists, measuring all aspects of the organization's processes, customers, and suppliers. The data is focused and comprehensive. Any data and information collected has a specific purpose known by the data collectors and generators.   □ □ □ □ □

3-19c   Information collected is timely, useful, accurate, and complete. Benchmark data exists for comparative purposes.   □ □ □ □ □

3-19d   Routine, periodic checks are made to ensure the validity of data and information collected.   □ □ □ □ □

3-19e   Appropriate, advanced technologies and tools are used in all data-and-information collection processes.   □ □ □ □ □

3-19f   All employees routinely use measures to identify problems. Quantitative methodologies identify solutions, and assessment techniques verify that remedies produce expected results.   □ □ □ □ □

3-19g   Qualitative data and information use appropriate technologies to identify improvement areas.   □ □ □ □ □

3-19h   Objectives have been established for production defects. Performance is measured and goals are being achieved.

□ □ □ □ □

3-19i   Quality measure includes parts per million (PPM) defect reporting and cost of quality reporting.

□ □ □ □ □

3-19j   Objectives have been established for production and supplier defects. Performance is measured, and goals are being achieved.

□ □ □ □ □

3-19k   Objectives have been set for cost of quality. Performance is measured, and goals are being achieved.

□ □ □ □ □

3-19l   Delivery measures include linearity of output and on-time deliveries.

□ □ □ □ □

3-19m   The following measures have been eliminated or deemphasized:

□ □ □ □ □

- labor efficiency (or derivations)
- machine utilization (or derivations)
- defects per person
- purchased part price variance
- manufacturing overhead rate

3-19n   Operating results are posted in a timely manner and made visible to company employees.

□ □ □ □ □

3-19o   Key measures are usually shown with additional information that points the way to improvements (e.g., run charts plus multi-level Pareto charts).

□ □ □ □ □

4—EXCELLENT
3—VERY GOOD
2—FAIR
1—POOR
0—NOT DONE

3-19p   Cost measures include inventory days on hand (or turns) and total asset turnover.

3-19q   Manufacturing cost-of-quality reports are presented as a routine part of management reporting. While it is difficult to obtain all costs of quality, at least the tangible numbers for appraisal, failure, and prevention are reported.

3-19r   The concept of cost of quality is understood in nonmanufacturing areas and reported when practical.

3-20 SETTING AND ATTAINING QUALITY GOALS

Short- and long-term quality goals that cause the organization to stretch are established, regularly reviewed, and monitored. These goals are targeted on improvements in total cost, cycle time (or response time), and customer quality requirements.

3-20a   Operational plans for achieving improved quality, improved response time, and reduced total cost goals carry clear priorities and accountability.

3-20b   A formal process for establishing these goals and plans exists and is followed.

4—EXCELLENT 3— VERY GOOD 2— FAIR 1—POOR 0—NOT DOING

3-20c Both intuition and quantitative information are used to identify areas of improvement. Benchmarking, customer requirements, process capability, and supplier requirements are regularly employed in this process.

3-20d Customers' expressed, expected, and exciting needs, gaps, and issues are integrated into the planning process for both products and processes.

3-20e Benchmark data establishing best-in-class practices are used to establish improvement planning for quality initiatives.

3-20f All levels of the organization participate in the improvement planning process.

3-20g Key requirements in technology, training and education, and supplier quality are regularly assessed and factored into the plans. Future targets and current status are part of the factoring and prioritizing process.

3-20h An evaluation of the planning process itself is periodically assessed and targeted for improvement and corrective action.

4

NEW PRODUCT DEVELOPMENT PROCESSES

QUALITATIVE CHARACTERISTICS

Class A All functions in the organization are involved with and actively support the product development process. Product requirements are derived from customer needs. Products are developed in significantly shorter time periods, meet these requirements, and require little or no support. Internal and external suppliers are involved and an active part of the development process. The resulting revenue and margins satisfy the projections of the original business plan proposals.

Class B Design engineering (or R&D) and other functions are involved in the development process. Product requirements are derived from customer needs. Product development times have been reduced. A low to medium level of support is required. Few design changes are required for products to meet the requirements.

Class C The product development process is primarily an engineering or R&D activity. Products are introduced close to schedule but contain traditional problems in manufacturing and the marketplace. Products require significant support to meet performance, quality, or operating objectives. The manufacturing process is not optimized for internal or external suppliers.

Some improvement in reducing development time has been achieved.

Class D   The products developed consistently do not meet schedule dates, performance, cost, quality, or reliability goals. They require high levels of support. There is little or no internal or external supplier involvement.

OVERVIEW ITEMS

4-1 COMMITMENT TO EXCELLENCE
An intense commitment to excel in the innovation, effectiveness, and speed of new product development is broadly shared by all levels of management throughout the organization.

4-2 MULTIFUNCTIONAL PRODUCT DEVELOPMENT TEAMS
Multifunctional product development teams—including manufacturing, marketing, finance, quality assurance, purchasing, suppliers, and, where appropriate, customers—are used during the design process for new product development.

4-3 EARLY TEAM INVOLVEMENT
Design for Manufacturability/Concurrent Engineering processes are utilized at the beginning and throughout the product development process.

4-4 CUSTOMER REQUIREMENTS USED TO DEVELOP PRODUCT SPECIFICATIONS
Customer requirements are determined utilizing processes such as Quality Function Deployment (QFD) and competitive benchmarking. These customer requirements are used to develop the specifications for the product.

4-5 DECREASE TIME-TO-MARKET

An ongoing effort to decrease the time-to-market—the elapsed time between the start of the design and the first shipment of the product—is viewed as an important competitive weapon, highly visible, and generating improvements.

4-6 PREFERRED COMPONENTS, MATERIALS, AND PROCESSES

There is an agreed-upon product development and manufacturing policy on commonality and use of preferred components and preferred processes in new designs.

4-7 EDUCATION AND TRAINING †

An active education and training process for all employees is in place focused on business and customer issues and improvements. Its objectives include Continuous Improvement, enhancing the empowered worker, flexibility, employment stability, and meeting future needs.

4-8 NEW PRODUCT DEVELOPMENT INTEGRATED WITH THE PLANNING AND CONTROL SYSTEM

All phases of new product development are integrated with the planning and control system.

4-9 PRODUCT DEVELOPMENT ACTIVITIES INTEGRATED WITH PLANNING AND CONTROL SYSTEM

Where applicable, product development activities in support of a customer order are integrated with the planning and control system.

4-10 CONTROLLING CHANGES

There is an effective process for evaluating, planning, and controlling changes to the existing products.

OVERVIEW AND DETAIL ITEMS

4-1 COMMITMENT TO EXCELLENCE*

An intense commitment to excel in the innovation, effectiveness, and speed of new product development is broadly shared by all levels of management throughout the organization.

4-2 MULTIFUNCTIONAL PRODUCT DEVELOPMENT TEAMS

Multifunctional product development teams— including manufacturing, marketing, finance, quality assurance, purchasing, suppliers, and, where appropriate, customers—are used during the design process for new product development.

4-2a   Multifunction team disciplines are utilized to plan, develop, and improve the effectiveness of new product development.

4-2b   All involved departments are considered part of the product development team. They are charged with the responsibility for creating high-quality products that are inexpensive to manufacture.

4-2c   Whenever possible, key suppliers are involved in the very early stages of new product development.

4-2d   Regular status meetings are held by the multifunctional development team on a weekly (or more frequent) basis. The focus is on status reporting by the core team members and selected other people from the extended team. Problem solving is managed off-line in working sessions.

4—EXCELLENT
3—VERY GOOD
2—FAIR
1—POOR
0—NOT DOING

4-2e   The costing system provides true and real costs to the development personnel. It is understood and supported by all functions, including cost and general accounting. Tools such as activity-based costing or activity-based management are utilized.

☐ ☐ ☐ ☐ ☐

4-3 EARLY TEAM INVOLVEMENT

Design for Manufacturability/Concurrent Engineering processes are utilized at the beginning and throughout the product development process.

☐ ☐ ☐ ☐ ☐

4-3a   Product development team objectives specifically include a broad set of requirements, including product performance, manufacturability, assembleability, testability, serviceability, high reliability, Just-in-Time manufacturing processes, etc.

☐ ☐ ☐ ☐ ☐

4-3b   Wherever possible, products and manufacturing processes are developed concurrently rather than sequentially.

☐ ☐ ☐ ☐ ☐

4-3c   Specific programs exist to develop and maintain a list of preferred suppliers, and to specify these suppliers in the development process.

☐ ☐ ☐ ☐ ☐

4-3d   Measurements are developed to evaluate product development processes; they include elements such as time-to-market, the number of total items, the number of processes, etc.

☐ ☐ ☐ ☐ ☐

4-4 CUSTOMER REQUIREMENTS USED TO DEVELOP PRODUCT SPECIFICATIONS

☐ ☐ ☐ ☐ ☐

Customer requirements are determined utilizing processes such as Quality Function Deployment (QFD) and competitive benchmarking. These customer requirements are used to develop the specifications for the product.

4-4a   The concepts of competitive bench-   ☐ ☐ ☐ ☐ ☐
marking and competitive analysis are understood and appropriately utilized.

4-4b   The concepts of Quality Function Deploy-   ☐ ☐ ☐ ☐ ☐
ment are understood and utilized, when appropriate, to determine customer and product requirements.

4-4c   Development teams and marketing people   ☐ ☐ ☐ ☐ ☐
can state their customers' "expressed" and "expected" needs.

4-4d   The concept of "exciting" customer needs   ☐ ☐ ☐ ☐ ☐
is understood, and efforts are underway to determine them in key areas.

4-5 DECREASE TIME-TO-MARKET

☐ ☐ ☐ ☐ ☐

An ongoing effort to decrease the time-to-market—the elapsed time between the start of the design and the first shipment of the product—is viewed as an important competitive weapon, highly visible, and generating improvements.

4—EXCELLENT 3—VERY GOOD 2—FAIR 1—POOR 0—NOT DOING

4-5a   There is a detailed product development
         schedule with authorization and funding to
         support each new product development
         project. Schedules are developed utilizing
         multifunctional inputs and commitments
         at the very beginning of the development.

4-5b   First-pass manufacturing yields are mea-
         sured and continuously and significantly
         improving for new products.

4-5c   Reliability of the product is demonstrated
         before first customer shipment and meets
         the product requirements.

4-6 PREFERRED COMPONENTS, MATERIALS, AND PROCESSES

*There is an agreed-upon product development
and manufacturing policy on commonality and
use of preferred components and preferred
processes in new designs.*

4-6a   A preferred components and processes list
         representing the requirements of design
         engineering, quality, manufacturing, and
         field service is available and utilized.

4-7 EDUCATION AND TRAINING †

*An active education and training process for all
employees is in place focused on business and
customer issues and improvements. Its objectives
include Continuous Improvement, enhancing the
empowered worker, flexibility, employment
stability, and meeting future needs.*

4—EXCELLENT
3—VERY GOOD
2—FAIR
1—POOR
0—NOT DOIN

4-7a   Management attitude and actions demonstrate a commitment to fully educate and train people prior to implementation of new technologies and processes. ☐ ☐ ☐ ☐ ☐

4-7b   Education is a participative process rather than a one-directional flow from the top of the organization to the bottom. ☐ ☐ ☐ ☐ ☐

4-7c   The education and training process recognizes people at all levels as experts in their areas, communicates objectives, and fully involves people in the process of changing their jobs. ☐ ☐ ☐ ☐ ☐

4-7d   The education and training approach is based on the principles of behavior change in an organization rather than merely a process of fact transfer regarding a specific technology. ☐ ☐ ☐ ☐ ☐

4-7e   The company has committed sufficient resources, financial and otherwise, to education and training. ☐ ☐ ☐ ☐ ☐

4-7f   An ongoing education and training process is used to refine and improve the use of business tools like team-based technologies, Just-in-Time (JIT), Total Quality Control (TQC), and Manufacturing Resource Planning system (MRP II), etc. ☐ ☐ ☐ ☐ ☐

4—EXCELLENT
3—VERY GOOD
2—FAIR
1—POOR
0—NOT DOING

4-8 NEW PRODUCT DEVELOPMENT INTEGRATED WITH THE PLANNING AND CONTROL SYSTEM

All phases of new product development are integrated with the planning and control system.

4-8a Once a new product is authorized, it is included in the sales and operations planning and master production scheduling processes.

4-8b The engineering and manufacturing scheduling systems are linked together, using a single set of numbers. Up-to-date due dates are communicated from the master production schedule through the scheduling system(s) to the engineering/ research and development work centers.

4-8c Managers within the product development areas understand the planning and scheduling system. They have accepted the responsibility for effectively using it.

4-8d As required, rough-cut capacity planning representing product engineering's capabilities is used to provide information for the sales and operations planning and master scheduling processes.

4-8e   For important product engineering work centers, predictions of the required capacity and measurements of actual output are provided by the planning and scheduling system. Managers use this information to ensure that a proper balance is achieved between the two.

☐ ☐ ☐ ☐ ☐

4-8f   When engineering/research and development schedules cannot be met, feedback is initiated so consequences can be determined. Causes of these delays are tracked and revised completion dates are provided.

☐ ☐ ☐ ☐ ☐

4-9 PRODUCT DEVELOPMENT ACTIVITIES INTEGRATED WITH PLANNING AND CONTROL SYSTEM

Where applicable, product development activities in support of a customer order are integrated with the planning and control system.

☐ ☐ ☐ ☐ ☐

4-9a   The product engineering and manufacturing scheduling systems are linked together, using a single set of numbers. Up-to-date due dates are communicated from the master production schedule through the scheduling system(s) to the engineering/research and development work centers.

☐ ☐ ☐ ☐ ☐

4—EXCELLENT 3—VERY GOOD 2—FAIR 1—POOR 0—NOT DOING

4-9b   Managers within product engineering/ research and development understand the planning and scheduling system. They have accepted the responsibility for effectively using it.

☐ ☐ ☐ ☐ ☐

4-9c   As required, rough-cut capacity planning representing engineering's capabilities is used to provide information for the sales and operations planning and master scheduling processes.

☐ ☐ ☐ ☐ ☐

4-9d   For important product engineering work centers, predictions of the required capacity and measurements of actual output are provided by the planning and scheduling system. Managers use this information to ensure that a proper balance is achieved between the two.

☐ ☐ ☐ ☐ ☐

4-9e   When product development schedules cannot be met, feedback is initiated so consequences can be determined. Causes of these delays are tracked and revised completion dates are provided.

☐ ☐ ☐ ☐ ☐

4-10 CONTROLLING CHANGES

☐ ☐ ☐ ☐ ☐

There is an effective process for evaluating, planning, and controlling changes to the existing products.

4—EXCELLENT
3—VERY GOOD
2—FAIR
1—POOR
0—NOT DONE

4-10a   A written engineering change policy is followed to ensure consistent and timely engineering changes.

☐ ☐ ☐ ☐ ☐

4-10b   The importance of engineering change coordination is reflected in the organization and reporting relationship of the engineering change coordination function.

☐ ☐ ☐ ☐ ☐

4-10c   Engineering changes are analyzed using Total Quality Control methods to reduce their number and associated costs.

☐ ☐ ☐ ☐ ☐

4-10d   The number of engineering changes for a product is used to measure the effectiveness of the product development process. Specific plans exist to eliminate the need for performance-related engineering changes by doing a more complete job of initial project design.

☐ ☐ ☐ ☐ ☐

4-10e   Engineering changes are effectively implemented using appropriate phase-in and phase-out techniques.

☐ ☐ ☐ ☐ ☐

5

PLANNING AND CONTROL PROCESSES

QUALITATIVE CHARACTERISTICS

Class A   Planning and control processes are effectively used company wide, from top to bottom. Their use generates significant improvements in customer service, productivity, inventory, and costs.

Class B   These processes are supported by top management and used by middle management to achieve measurable company improvements.

Class C   Planning and control system is operated primarily as a better method for ordering materials; contributing to better inventory management.

Class D   Information provided by the planning and control system is inaccurate and poorly understood by users; providing little help in running the business.

OVERVIEW ITEMS

5-1 COMMITMENT TO EXCELLENCE
There is a commitment by top management and throughout the company to use effective planning and control techniques—providing a single set of numbers used by all members of the organization. These numbers represent valid schedules that people believe and use to run the business.

5-2 SALES AND OPERATIONS PLANNING
There is a sales and operations planning process in place that maintains a valid, current operating plan in support of customer requirements and the business plan. This process includes a formal meeting each month run by the general manager and covers a planning horizon adequate to plan resources effectively.

5-3 FINANCIAL PLANNING, REPORTING, AND MEASUREMENT
There is a single set of numbers used by all functions within the operating system, which provides the source data used for financial planning, reporting, and measurement.

5-4 "WHAT IF" SIMULATIONS
"What if" simulations are used to evaluate alternative operating plans and develop contingency plans for materials, people, equipment, and finances.

5-5 ACCOUNTABLE FORECASTING PROCESS
There is a process for forecasting all anticipated demands with sufficient detail and adequate planning horizon to support business plan-

ning, sales and operations planning, and master production scheduling. Forecast accuracy is measured in order to continuously improve the process.

5-6 SALES PLANS

There is a formal sales planning process in place with the sales force responsible and accountable for developing and executing the resulting sales plan. Differences between the sales plan and the forecast are reconciled.

5-7 INTEGRATED CUSTOMER ORDER ENTRY AND PROMISING

Customer order entry and promising are integrated with the master production scheduling system and inventory data. There are mechanisms for matching incoming orders to forecasts and for handling abnormal demands.

5-8 MASTER PRODUCTION SCHEDULING

The master production scheduling process is perpetually managed in order to ensure a balance of stability and responsiveness. The master production schedule is reconciled with the production plan resulting from the sales and operations planning process.

5-9 MATERIAL PLANNING AND CONTROL

There is a material planning process that maintains valid schedules and a material control process that communicates priorities through a manufacturing schedule, dispatch list, supplier schedule, and/or a kanban mechanism.

5-10 SUPPLIER PLANNING AND CONTROL

A supplier planning and scheduling process provides visibility for key items covering an adequate planning horizon.

5-11 CAPACITY PLANNING AND CONTROL

There is a capacity planning process using rough-cut capacity planning and, where applicable, capacity requirements planning in which planned capacity, based on demonstrated output, is balanced with required capacity. A capacity control process is used to measure and manage factory throughput and queues.

5-12 CUSTOMER SERVICE

An objective for on-time deliveries exists, and the customers are in agreement with it. Performance against the objective is measured.

5-13 SALES PLAN PERFORMANCE

Accountability for performance to the sales plan has been established, and the method of measurement and the goal has been agreed upon.

5-14 PRODUCTION PLAN PERFORMANCE

Accountability for production plan performance has been established, and the method of measurement and the goal has been agreed upon. Production plan performance is more than ± 2 percent of the monthly plan, except in cases where midmonth changes have been authorized by top management.

5-15 MASTER PRODUCTION SCHEDULE PERFORMANCE

Accountability for master production schedule performance has been established, and the method of measurement and the goal has been agreed upon. Master production schedule performance is 95–100 percent of the plan.

5-16 MANUFACTURING SCHEDULE PERFORMANCE

Accountability for manufacturing schedule performance has been established, and the method of measurement and the goal has been agreed upon. Manufacturing schedule performance is 95–100 percent of the plan.

5-17 SUPPLIER DELIVERY PERFORMANCE

Accountability for supplier delivery performance has been established, and the method of measurement and the goal agreed upon. Supplier delivery performance is 95–100 percent of the plan.

5-18 BILL OF MATERIAL STRUCTURE AND ACCURACY

The planning and control process is supported by a properly structured, accurate, and integrated set of bills of material (formulas, recipes) and related data. Bill of material accuracy is in the 98–100 percent range.

5-19 INVENTORY RECORD ACCURACY

There is an inventory control process in place that provides accurate warehouse, stockroom, and work-in-process inventory data. At least 95 percent of all item inventory records match the physical counts, within the counting tolerance.

5-20 ROUTING ACCURACY

When routings are applicable, there is a development and maintenance process in place that provides accurate routing information. Routing accuracy is in the 95–100 percent range.

5-21 EDUCATION AND TRAINING†

An active education and training process for all employees is in place focused on business and customer issues and improvements. Its objectives include Continuous Improvement, enhancing the empowered worker, flexibility, employment stability, and meeting future needs.

5-22 DISTRIBUTION RESOURCE PLANNING (DRP)

Distribution Resource Planning, where applicable, is utilized to manage the logistics of distribution. DRP information is used for sales and operations planning, master production scheduling, supplier scheduling, transportation planning, and the scheduling of shipping.

OVERVIEW AND DETAIL ITEMS

4—EXCELLENT 3—VERY GOOD 2—FAIR 1—POOR 0—NOT DOING

5-1 COMMITMENT TO EXCELLENCE*

☐ ☐ ☐ ☐ ☐

There is a commitment by top management and throughout the company to use effective planning and control techniques—providing a single set of numbers used by all members of the organization. These numbers represent valid schedules that people believe and use to run the business.

5-2 SALES AND OPERATIONS PLANNING

☐ ☐ ☐ ☐ ☐

There is a sales and operations planning process in place that maintains a valid, current operating plan in support of customer requirements and the business plan. This process includes a formal meeting each month run by the general manager and covers a planning horizon adequate to plan resources effectively.

4—EXCELLENT 3—VERY GOOD 2—FAIR 1—POOR 0—NOT DOING

5-2a   There is a concise written sales and operations planning policy that covers the purpose, process, and participants in the process.

5-2b   Sales and operations planning is truly a process and not just a meeting. There is a sequence of steps that are laid out and followed.

5-2c   The meeting dates are set well ahead to avoid schedule conflicts. In case of an emergency and the department manager is unable to attend the meeting, he or she is represented by someone who is empowered to speak for the department.

5-2d   A formal agenda is circulated prior to the meeting.

5-2e   For each product family, plans are reviewed in units of measure that communicate most effectively.

5-2f   The new product development schedule is reviewed at the sales and operations planning meeting.

5-2g   All participants come prepared to the sales and operations planning meeting. There are preliminary meetings by department: Sales and Marketing to prepare a Sales Plan, Design Engineering to prepare a New Product Plan, Manufacturing to prepare a Production Plan.

4—EXCELLENT 3—VERY GOOD 2—FAIR 1—POOR 0—NOT DOIN'

5-2h   The presentation of information includes a review of both past performances and future plans for: sales, production, inventory, backlog, shipments, and new product activity. □ □ □ □ □

5-2i   Inventory and/or delivery lead time (backlog) strategies are reviewed each month as part of the process. □ □ □ □ □

5-2j   There is a process of reviewing and documenting assumptions about the business and the marketplace. This is to enhance the understanding of the business and represents the basis for future projections. □ □ □ □ □

5-2k   Sales and operations planning is an action process. Conflicts are resolved and decisions are made, communicated, and implemented. □ □ □ □ □

5-2l   Any large and/or unanticipated changes are communicated to other departments prior to the meeting in order to minimize surprises in the meeting. □ □ □ □ □

5-2m   Minutes of the meeting are circulated immediately after the meeting. This is typically done within twenty-four hours of the meeting. □ □ □ □ □

5-2n   The mechanism is in place to ensure that aggregate sales plans agree with detailed sales plans by item and by market segment or territory. There is a consensus from sales, marketing, and operating management. □ □ □ □ □

5-2o Time fences have been established as guidelines for managing changes. In the near-term, there is an effort to minimize the changes in order to gain the benefits of stability. In the mid-term range, priority changes are expected but are reviewed to ensure they can be executed. In the long-term, less precision is expected but direction is established.

☐ ☐ ☐ ☐ ☐

5-2p Tolerances are established to determine acceptable performance for: sales, design engineering, finance, and production. They are reviewed and updated. Accountability is clearly established.

☐ ☐ ☐ ☐ ☐

5-2q The master production schedules for a family of products are summed and checked for agreement with the production plan for that family. The sum of the master production schedules for a family of items is constrained by the production plan for that family.

☐ ☐ ☐ ☐ ☐

5-2r There is an ongoing critique of the sales and operations planning process.

☐ ☐ ☐ ☐ ☐

5-3 FINANCIAL PLANNING, REPORTING, AND MEASUREMENT

☐ ☐ ☐ ☐ ☐

There is a single set of numbers used by all functions within the operating system, which provides the source data used for financial planning, reporting, and measurement.

4—EXCELLENT
3—VERY GOOD
2—FAIR
1—POOR
0—NOT DOIN

5-3a   The financial projections developed in the sales and operations planning process are linked to the company's financial plans. When financial projections differ from the financial plans contained in the business plan, the differences are reconciled and either the sales and operations plan or the business plan is updated in order to measure performance.   ☐ ☐ ☐ ☐ ☐

5-3b   The finance department uses the same source data as other departments for sales, shipments, and any other operating system information.   ☐ ☐ ☐ ☐ ☐

5-3c   The finance department recognizes the limitations of traditional performance measurements, particularly those related to overhead allocation, and understands when and how those methods may produce misleading or incorrect data. Financial measurements, particularly those related to overhead allocation, have been reviewed and updated as necessary to support Just-in-Time practices.   ☐ ☐ ☐ ☐ ☐

5-3d   All financial systems (billing, accounts payable, cost accounting, purchasing, receiving, inventory, etc.) are fully integrated with all transaction systems.   ☐ ☐ ☐ ☐ ☐

5-3e   Accounts payable, purchasing, and receiving tie to material receipt transactions.   ☐ ☐ ☐ ☐ ☐

	4—EXCELLENT	3—VERY GOOD	2—FAIR	1—POOR	0—NOT DOING

5-3f Labor reporting, either in the form of transactions or in the form of an allocation of labor hours, is used to determine the cost of the product.

☐ ☐ ☐ ☐ ☐

5-3g Where work orders are used, work order closing transactions are used to generate movement of inventory from one account to another in the general ledger and also to trigger variance reports for cost accounting purposes.

☐ ☐ ☐ ☐ ☐

5-3h Customer order shipment transactions drive the updating of finished goods inventory and the billing system at the same time.

☐ ☐ ☐ ☐ ☐

5-3i A cash-flow plan is prepared using the numbers from the operating system. The plan covers the sales and operation planning horizon, is reviewed at least monthly, and revised as changes occur.

☐ ☐ ☐ ☐ ☐

5-3j Simulation tools are actively used to convert operating data into financial data quickly for the purpose of simulation testing, decision making, and contingency planning.

☐ ☐ ☐ ☐ ☐

5-3k The finance department is proactive in simplifying all financial processes (e.g., cost accounting system) and eliminating nonvalue-added activities.

☐ ☐ ☐ ☐ ☐

4—EXCELLENT *3—VERY GOOD* *2—FAIR* *1—POOR* *0—NOT DONE*

☐ ☐ ☐ ☐ ☐

5-4 "WHAT IF" SIMULATIONS
*"What if" simulations are used to evaluate
alternative operating plans and develop
contingency plans for materials, people,
equipment, and finances.*

5-4a   There is a computer-based simulation pro- ☐ ☐ ☐ ☐ ☐
cess supporting sales and operations plan-
ning that permits the evaluation of various
levels of demand, supply, production, inventory, and/or backlogs.

5-4b   There is a simulation capability used to ☐ ☐ ☐ ☐ ☐
support customer-order entry and promis-
ing in determining the effects of making
unplanned customer promises.

5-4c   Rough-cut capacity planning is used to ☐ ☐ ☐ ☐ ☐
evaluate the impact on critical resources of
alternative production and master production schedule plans.

5-4d   Where applicable, capacity requirements ☐ ☐ ☐ ☐ ☐
planning is used to evaluate detailed capacity constraints when planning and bud-
geting labor and equipment needs.

5-4e   Where applicable, Material Requirements ☐ ☐ ☐ ☐ ☐
Planning and Distribution Requirements
Planning are utilized to evaluate alternate
planning factors (e.g., lot size, safety
stock, lead time, etc.) and the resultant
impact on inventory levels.

5-5 ACCOUNTABLE FORECASTING PROCESS

☐ ☐ ☐ ☐ ☐

There is a process for forecasting all anticipated demands with sufficient detail and adequate planning horizon to support business planning, sales and operations planning, and master production scheduling. Forecast accuracy is measured in order to continuously improve the process.

5-5a There is clear accountability for developing the forecast, and the importance of this effort is reflected in the organization and reporting relationship of the forecasting function.

☐ ☐ ☐ ☐ ☐

5-5b The forecaster (frequently called the demand planner or manager) understands the product, the customer base, the marketplace, and the manufacturing system.

☐ ☐ ☐ ☐ ☐

5-5c All demands are included in the forecast, e.g., spares, samples, internal use, etc.

☐ ☐ ☐ ☐ ☐

5-5d Available statistical forecasting tools are utilized when and where applicable.

☐ ☐ ☐ ☐ ☐

5-5e Spare parts and other lower-level demands are handled with a forecasting system and appropriate order-entry mechanism that introduces the demands at the right level in the detailed material planning process.

☐ ☐ ☐ ☐ ☐

5-5f   Detailed forecasts are reconciled with aggregate forecasts and communicated to the
master production scheduler and sales
force.

5-5g   The significant assumptions underlying
the forecast are documented. They are reviewed at least monthly and updated as
market conditions change.

5-5h   The forecaster participates in the product
management and product development
processes, including product structuring.

5-5i   Both aggregate and detailed measurements
of forecast accuracy are used to improve
the process.

5-6 SALES PLANS

*There is a formal sales planning process in place
with the sales force responsible and accountable
for developing and executing the resulting sales
plan. Differences between the sales plan and the
forecast are reconciled.*

5-6a   The sales force understands the impact of
sales planning on the company's ability to
satisfy its customers.

5-6b   Actual sales are measured against sales
plans. Measurements are broken down into
sales responsibility areas.

4—EXCELLENT 3—VERY GOOD 2—FAIR 1—POOR 0—NOT DOING

5-6c The sales planning process is designed in such a way as to minimize the administrative impact for the sales force. ☐ ☐ ☐ ☐ ☐

5-6d The incentives of the sales compensation system are effective and do not inject bias into the sales plan and forecast. ☐ ☐ ☐ ☐ ☐

5-6e Where applicable, the sales force is actively pursuing customer linking. The customer's planning systems are linked with the company's to provide visibility of future demands. ☐ ☐ ☐ ☐ ☐

5-6f Aggregate forecasts are reconciled with the sales plan. ☐ ☐ ☐ ☐ ☐

5-6g Sales participates with marketing, forecasting, and manufacturing in a demand planning meeting to prepare for each sales and operations planning meeting. A system is in use to communicate customer intelligence information to forecasting. ☐ ☐ ☐ ☐ ☐

5-6h Sales areas are provided with useful feedback regarding their performance to plan at least monthly. Sales plans are stated so that they are meaningful to the sales force yet translate into the sales and operations process. ☐ ☐ ☐ ☐ ☐

5-6i The assumptions underlying the sales plan are documented. They are reviewed on a regular basis and changed as necessary. ☐ ☐ ☐ ☐ ☐

4—EXCELLENT
3—VERY GOOD
2—FAIR
1—POOR
0—NOT DOING

☐ ☐ ☐ ☐ ☐

5-7 INTEGRATED CUSTOMER ORDER ENTRY AND PROMISING

Customer order entry and promising are integrated with the master production scheduling system and inventory data. There are mechanisms for matching incoming orders to forecasts and for handling abnormal demands.

5-7a   The order promising function has access to appropriate and timely information, such as Available-to-Promise (ATP), to ensure that good promises can be made. Where manufacturing times have been reduced such that production is based on actual customer orders, order promising would be based on the rate of production for the family of products. Otherwise, order promising would be based on the Available-to-Promise calculation for each item.

☐ ☐ ☐ ☐ ☐

5-7b   Sales and marketing participate in developing appropriate time fences for managing change.

☐ ☐ ☐ ☐ ☐

5-7c   There is a process in place for identifying and managing abnormal demands.

☐ ☐ ☐ ☐ ☐

5-7d   Abnormal demand (both active and history) is coded properly in the data base.

☐ ☐ ☐ ☐ ☐

5-7e   Customer orders are processed on a timely basis. The number of customer orders awaiting processing is measured and managed.

☐ ☐ ☐ ☐ ☐

4—EXCELLENT 3—VERY GOOD 2—FAIR 1—POOR 0—NOT DOING

5-7f   Order-entry errors are measured and man- □ □ □ □ □
aged to eliminate the causes of the errors.

5-7g   The number of customer-initiated sales □ □ □ □ □
change orders is measured and managed to
an acceptable level.

5-8 MASTER PRODUCTION SCHEDULING □ □ □ □ □

*The master production scheduling process is
perpetually managed in order to ensure a
balance of stability and responsiveness. The
master production schedule is reconciled with the
production plan resulting from the sales and
operations planning process.*

5-8a   Accountability for maintaining the master □ □ □ □ □
schedule is clear. The importance of mas-
ter scheduling is reflected in the organization and reporting relationship of the
master scheduling function.

5-8b   The master scheduler understands the □ □ □ □ □
product, manufacturing process, manufacturing planning and control system, and
the needs of the marketplace.

5-8c   The master scheduler participates in and □ □ □ □ □
provides important detail information to
the sales and operations planning process.

5-8d   The master scheduler responds to feed- □ □ □ □ □
back that identifies master schedule
impacting material and/or capacity availability problems by initiating the problem-
resolution process.

4—EXCELLENT
3—VERY GOOD
2—FAIR
1—POOR
0—NOT DONE

5-8e   Planning bills of material (if used) are maintained jointly by the master scheduler and sales and marketing.

☐ ☐ ☐ ☐ ☐

5-8f   A written master schedule policy is followed to monitor stability and responsiveness; goals are established and measured.

☐ ☐ ☐ ☐ ☐

5-8g   The master schedule is "firmed up" over a sufficient horizon to enable stability of operations. Guidelines for this firmed horizon include:

☐ ☐ ☐ ☐ ☐

1. cumulative material lead time
2. lead time to planned capacity
3. lead time to cover customer order backlog (order book)

5-8h   Master schedule changes within the "firm zone" (closest time fence) are managed; they are authorized by the appropriate people, measured, and reviewed for cause.

☐ ☐ ☐ ☐ ☐

5-8i   Policy governs the use of safety stock and/or option overplanning used to increase responsiveness and compensate for inconsistent supply and/or demand variations.

☐ ☐ ☐ ☐ ☐

5-8j   The master schedule is summarized appropriately and reconciled with the agreed to production rate (production plan) from the sales and operations planning process.

☐ ☐ ☐ ☐ ☐

5-8k   All levels of master scheduled items are identified and master scheduled.

☐ ☐ ☐ ☐ ☐

5-8l The master schedule is in weekly, daily, or smaller periods, may be rate-based, and replanned at least weekly.

☐ ☐ ☐ ☐ ☐

5-8m The structure of the bills of material supports the master scheduling/forecasting process.

☐ ☐ ☐ ☐ ☐

5-8n Forecast consumption processes are used to prevent planning nervousness.

☐ ☐ ☐ ☐ ☐

5-8o The alternative approaches used with planning bills of material to develop production forecasts for master scheduled items are well understood and an appropriate process is used.

☐ ☐ ☐ ☐ ☐

5-8p Rough-cut capacity planning, or its equivalent, is used to evaluate the impact of significant master schedule changes on critical resources. Demonstrated capacity is measured and compared to required capacity.

☐ ☐ ☐ ☐ ☐

5-8q A finishing/final assembly mechanism or kanban approach is coordinated with the master schedule to schedule customer orders to completion or replenish finished goods.

☐ ☐ ☐ ☐ ☐

5-8r Where applicable, mixed-model master scheduling is being used.

☐ ☐ ☐ ☐ ☐

5-8s A weekly master schedule communications meeting exists and is attended by all using functions.

☐ ☐ ☐ ☐ ☐

4—EXCELLENT 3—VERY GOOD 2—FAIR 1—POOR 0—NOT DONE

5-8t   The linearity of output is measured; the
graphic illustration of results should reflect
daily performance to a planned linear output; reasons for deviations are highlighted
with appropriate analysis.

5-9 MATERIAL PLANNING AND CONTROL

*There is a material planning process that
maintains valid schedules and a material control
process that communicates priorities through a
manufacturing schedule, dispatch list, supplier
schedule, and/or a kanban mechanism.*

Material Planning and Material Control

5-9a   Material planners and schedulers understand the product, the manufacturing process, the manufacturing planning and
control system, and are accountable for
maintaining a valid plan.

5-9b   All involved employees—including planners, production people, buyers, etc.—
operate under the "silence is approval"
principle and are responsible to feed
back schedule problems that cannot be
resolved.

4—EXCELLENT
3—VERY GOOD
2—FAIR
1—POOR
0—NOT DOING

5-9c   Planners are responsible for maintaining, periodically reviewing, and analyzing the accuracy and validity of all appropriate planning parameters such as order quantities or lot sizes, lead times, queues, safety stocks, etc.

☐ ☐ ☐ ☐ ☐

5-9d   Production supervisors and buyers understand and use the system and are accountable for maintaining data integrity on information under their responsibility (e.g., point-of-use inventory, planning parameters and schedule, or order file data, etc.).

☐ ☐ ☐ ☐ ☐

5-9e   There are formal communication processes among planning, production, and purchasing for the purpose of exchanging the information needed to maintain a valid schedule. The frequency and format (meetings, reports, calls) is determined by the situation.

☐ ☐ ☐ ☐ ☐

5-9f   The informal priority systems (shortage list, hot list, priority codes, etc.) have been eliminated, and there is only one priority setting mechanism.

☐ ☐ ☐ ☐ ☐

5-9g   MRP time periods are weekly or smaller to provide appropriate resolution of priorities.

☐ ☐ ☐ ☐ ☐

5-9h   The MRP system is run as frequently as required to maintain valid schedules. Daily may be required, but weekly processing is a minimum.

☐ ☐ ☐ ☐ ☐

4—EXCELLENT 3—VERY GOOD 2—FAIR 1—POOR 0—NOT DONE

5-9i The system uses standard logic to generate action/exception messages, including Need to Release Order, Need to Reschedule Order, Need to Cancel Order, Due Date, Past Due, or Release Past Due.   ☐ ☐ ☐ ☐ ☐

5-9j The system has a firm planned order capability that is used, when necessary, to override the suggested plan.   ☐ ☐ ☐ ☐ ☐

5-9k In reconciling problems, the planners bottom-up replan using single-level pegging to identify the source of demand.   ☐ ☐ ☐ ☐ ☐

5-9l The system has an effective component availability checking mechanism and the planners use it to determine the feasibility of releasing an order or schedule.   ☐ ☐ ☐ ☐ ☐

5-9m When applicable, the system includes the capability to alter the bill of material for an individual order when necessary to handle temporary substitutions, etc.   ☐ ☐ ☐ ☐ ☐

5-9n All action/exception messages are prioritized, reviewed, and problems are acted upon in a timely manner.   ☐ ☐ ☐ ☐ ☐

5-9o The number of action/exception messages for each planner is monitored for activity and trends.   ☐ ☐ ☐ ☐ ☐

5-9p Where work orders are used, the volume of reschedules is tracked to monitor the stability of the plan and to determine the causes of excessive rescheduling activity.   ☐ ☐ ☐ ☐ ☐

5-9q   Where work orders are used, orders are released with full material availability and full lead time 95–100 percent of the time.

Shop Floor Control (where applicable)

5-9r   Production management is accountable to meet operation due dates.

5-9s   The dispatch list is the only priority tool, and operation due and start dates are the only priority techniques used.

5-9t   The system includes a detailed scheduling capability to create start and due dates on a work order and operations within a routing.

5-9u   The system includes the capability to modify all start and due dates on a work order and operations within a routing.

5-9v   The system includes the capability to report status by operation.

5-9w   An anticipated-delay reporting process is used to maintain due date validity.

5-9x   The system includes a dispatch list by work center that shows item number, order number, order quantity, operation number, operation start and due date, and order due date.

4—EXCELLENT 3—VERY GOOD 2—FAIR 1—POOR 0—NOT DOI

5-10 SUPPLIER PLANNING AND CONTROL

A supplier planning and scheduling process provides visibility for key items covering an adequate planning horizon.

5-10a At least 80 percent of the suppliers have been educated in MRP II and/or JIT and understand the supplier scheduling process.

5-10b Suppliers agree to plan raw material and capacity to meet the requirements displayed on the supplier schedule.

5-10c There is a clear policy statement of the respective responsibilities of the supplier scheduler and buyer, including at what point each becomes involved in problem resolution.

5-10d The supplier schedule displays planned orders and/or scheduled receipts over the planning horizon for all items provided by the supplier.

5-10e Commitment zones are established in the supplier schedule representing firm commitments, material commitments, and capacity planning commitments.

5-10f Time periods on the supplier schedule are weeks or smaller for at least the first four weeks displayed.

5-10g The supplier scheduler and/or buyers meet with production planners as frequently as required to maintain a valid schedule.

□ □ □ □ □

5-10h The suppliers understand the principle behind "silence is approval" and agree to notify the buyer in advance if a due date will be missed.

□ □ □ □ □

5-10i Supplier schedules are communicated to suppliers at least weekly.

□ □ □ □ □

5-10j For nonsupplier schedule items, 95 percent of purchase orders are released with full lead time.

□ □ □ □ □

5-10k There is a purchasing policy that states the set of criteria that defines "key" items, which are planned and scheduled through a supplier scheduling process. Typical considerations include factors such as 80 percent of purchase content, long lead times, critical items, etc.

□ □ □ □ □

5-11 CAPACITY PLANNING AND CONTROL

□ □ □ □ □

There is a capacity planning process using rough-cut capacity planning and, where applicable, capacity requirements planning in which planned capacity, based on demonstrated output, is balanced with required capacity. A capacity control process is used to measure and manage factory throughput and queues.

Capacity Planning and Capacity Control

4—EXCELLENT
3—VERY GOOD
2—FAIR
1—POOR
0—NOT DOING

5-11a   Capacity planning is well understood by all appropriate personnel and used to plan labor and machinery requirements.

☐ ☐ ☐ ☐ ☐

5-11b   There is an understanding of the respective responsibilities of the capacity planner and production supervisor in the capacity management process (e.g., accountability for maintaining the accuracy of production-oriented capacity planning parameters such as planned capacity, number of workers and/or machines, number of shifts).

☐ ☐ ☐ ☐

5-11c   Production supervisors and capacity planners meet at least weekly to resolve capacity issues.

☐ ☐ ☐ ☐ ☐

5-11d   All activities that consume capacity are considered in developing the capacity requirement (e.g., maintenance, engineering projects, customized parts, etc.).

☐ ☐ ☐ ☐ ☐

5-11e   Where applicable, other constraints such as engineering and supplier capacity are considered in the capacity management process.

☐ ☐ ☐ ☐ ☐

5-11f   Work centers are appropriately defined to enable control of priorities and capacities while minimizing data maintenance, transactions, and reports.

☐ ☐ ☐ ☐ ☐

5-11g   A "Load Factor" that recognizes capacity loss due to utilization, efficiency, and absenteeism is maintained and used in projecting capacity.

☐ ☐ ☐ ☐ ☐

4—EXCELLENT
3—VERY GOOD
2—FAIR
1—POOR
0—NOT DOING

5-11h   Corrective action is taken to address overdue capacity requirements caused by past
due orders.

5-11i   The capacity planning process includes
appropriate productivity analysis.

Capacity Requirements Planning (where applicable)

5-11j   System produces capacity requirements
summary report by work center and a detailed capacity report.

5-11k   Data used by the capacity planning system
is audited for accuracy. This includes capacity planning parameters such as demonstrated capacity, planned capacity (both
with reasonable tolerance), number of
workers/machines, number of shifts, number of hours per shift, etc.

5-11l   Process includes variance analysis of
planned and actual input, output, and
queue levels (Input/Output Report).

The following items are key performance measurements of planning and control processes. See Appendix A for the preferred method of calculating the following performance measurements; see Appendix B for supplemental measurements.

4—EXCELLENT 3—VERY GOOD 2—FAIR 1—POOR 0—NOT DOING

5-12 CUSTOMER SERVICE

An objective for on-time deliveries exists, and the customers are in agreement with it. Performance against the objective is measured.

5-12a   Delivery to first promise and/or line item fill rate is at least 95 percent; higher is required by the customers.

5-12b   Graphs or charts showing the distribution of shipments about the promised date (target date) are maintained along with appropriate analysis, highlighting the primary causes of deviation.

5-13 SALES PLAN PERFORMANCE*

Accountability for performance to the sales plan has been established, and the method of measurement and the goal has been agreed upon.

5-14 PRODUCTION PLAN PERFORMANCE*

Accountability for production plan performance has been established, and the method of measurement and the goal has been agreed upon. Production plan performance is more than ±2 percent of the monthly plan, except in cases where midmonth changes have been authorized by top management.

4—EXCELLENT 3—VERY GOOD 2—FAIR 1—POOR 0—NOT DOING

☐ ☐ ☐ ☐ ☐

5-15 MASTER PRODUCTION SCHEDULE PERFORMANCE*

Accountability for master production schedule performance has been established, and the method of measurement and the goal has been agreed upon. Master production schedule performance is 95–100 percent of the plan.

☐ ☐ ☐ ☐ ☐

5-16 MANUFACTURING SCHEDULE PERFORMANCE*

Accountability for manufacturing schedule performance has been established, and the method of measurement and the goal has been agreed upon. Manufacturing schedule performance is 95–100 percent of the plan.

☐ ☐ ☐ ☐ ☐

5-17 SUPPLIER DELIVERY PERFORMANCE*

Accountability for supplier delivery performance has been established, and the method of measurement and the goal agreed upon. Supplier delivery performance is 95–100 percent of the plan.

☐ ☐ ☐ ☐ ☐

5-18 BILL OF MATERIAL STRUCTURE AND ACCURACY

The planning and control process is supported by a properly structured, accurate, and integrated set of bills of material (formulas, recipes) and related data. Bill of material accuracy is in the 98–100 percent range.

4—EXCELLENT   3—VERY GOOD   2—FAIR   1—POOR   0—NOT DONE

5-18a   Responsibility and accountability for developing and maintaining bills of material are clearly defined in written policy.

☐ ☐ ☐ ☐ ☐

5-18b   All functions that use the bills of materials participate in their structuring.

☐ ☐ ☐ ☐ ☐

5-18c   Bills of material are properly structured, represent the way products are built, and support the planning and control processes.

☐ ☐ ☐ ☐ ☐

5-18d   There is a bill of material accuracy audit process in place. This process examines the bill of material at a single level, looking for correct components, quantity per, and component unit of measure.

☐ ☐ ☐ ☐ ☐

5-18e   Audit results show the bills of material to be in the 98–100 percent range.

☐ ☐ ☐ ☐ ☐

5-18f   Finance uses the bill of material in costing the product.

☐ ☐ ☐ ☐ ☐

5-18g   There is a policy and procedure in place that identifies who is responsible for loading and maintaining each field of the item master file.

☐ ☐ ☐ ☐ ☐

5-19 INVENTORY RECORD ACCURACY   ☐ ☐ ☐ ☐ ☐
There is an inventory control process in place that provides accurate warehouse, stockroom, and work-in-process inventory data. At least 95 percent of all item inventory records match the physical counts, within the counting tolerance.

4—EXCELLENT 3—VERY GOOD 2—FAIR 1—POOR 0—NOT DOING

5-19a   Accountability for maintaining accurate inventory records is clearly understood by all those controlling inventories. This includes raw materials, finished goods, work-in-process, and point-of-use inventory.

☐ ☐ ☐ ☐ ☐

5-19b   Cycle counting procedures are used to identify and resolve inventory errors and measure inventory accuracy.

☐ ☐ ☐ ☐ ☐

5-19c   The cycle counting process has replaced the periodic physical inventory.

☐ ☐ ☐ ☐ ☐

5-19d   Cycle count results show the inventory records to be in the 95–100 percent range.

☐ ☐ ☐ ☐ ☐

5-20 ROUTING ACCURACY

☐ ☐ ☐ ☐ ☐

When routings are applicable, there is a development and maintenance process in place that provides accurate routing information. Routing accuracy is in the 95–100 percent range.

5-20a   There is a written policy that clearly identifies responsibility and accountability for developing and maintaining routings.

☐ ☐ ☐ ☐ ☐

5-20b   All functions that use the routings participate in their development.

☐ ☐ ☐ ☐ ☐

5-20c   The routings represent the way products are made and are integrated with the bills of materials.

☐ ☐ ☐ ☐ ☐

4—EXCELLENT
3—VERY GOOD
2—FAIR
1—POOR
0—NOT DONE

5-20d   There is a routing accuracy audit process in place. This process examines the routings for proper sequence of operations, work center number, missing or unnecessary operations, and, with tolerance, set-up and run times.

☐ ☐ ☐ ☐ ☐

5-20e   Audit results show the routings to be in the 95–100 percent range.

☐ ☐ ☐ ☐ ☐

5-20f   Finance uses the routing in costing the product.

☐ ☐ ☐ ☐ ☐

5-21   EDUCATION AND TRAINING†

☐ ☐ ☐ ☐ ☐

An active education and training process for all employees is in place focused on business and customer issues and improvements. Its objectives include Continuous Improvement, enhancing the empowered worker, flexibility, employment stability, and meeting future needs.

5-21a   Management attitude and actions demonstrate a commitment to fully educate and train people prior to implementation of new technologies and processes.

☐ ☐ ☐ ☐ ☐

5-21b   Education is a participative process rather than a one-directional flow from the top of the organization to the bottom.

☐ ☐ ☐ ☐ ☐

5-21c   The education and training process recognizes people at all levels as experts in their areas, communicates objectives, and fully involves people in the process of changing their jobs.

☐ ☐ ☐ ☐ ☐

4—EXCELLENT 3—VERY GOOD 2—FAIR 1—POOR 0—NOT DOING

5-21d The education and training approach is based on the principles of behavior change in an organization rather than merely a process of fact transfer regarding a specific technology.

☐ ☐ ☐ ☐ ☐

5-21e The company has committed sufficient resources, financial and otherwise, to education and training.

☐ ☐ ☐ ☐ ☐

5-21f An ongoing education and training process is used to refine and improve the use of business tools like team-based technologies, Just-in-Time (JIT), Total Quality Control (TQC), Manufacturing Resource Planning system (MRP II), etc.

☐ ☐ ☐ ☐ ☐

5-21g Areas of employee improvement needs are continuously assessed.

☐ ☐ ☐ ☐ ☐

5-22 DISTRIBUTION RESOURCE PLANNING (DRP)

☐ ☐ ☐ ☐ ☐

Distribution Resource Planning, where applicable, is utilized to manage the logistics of distribution. DRP information is used for sales and operations planning, master production scheduling, supplier scheduling, transportation planning, and the scheduling of shipping.

5-22a There is a concise written Distribution Resource Planning policy that covers purpose, process, and participants.

☐ ☐ ☐ ☐ ☐

5-22b　Distribution requirements are considered and reconciled through the sales and operations planning and master production scheduling processes.　☐ ☐ ☐ ☐ ☐

5-22c　The distribution network maintained in the DRP system is complete; it reflects which items are stocked at each distribution center.　☐ ☐ ☐ ☐ ☐

5-22d　Forecasts are available for each stock-keeping unit in each distribution center.　☐ ☐ ☐ ☐ ☐

5-22e　Time periods for DRP are weeks or smaller.　☐ ☐ ☐ ☐ ☐

5-22f　Distribution Resource Planning is run weekly or more frequently.　☐ ☐ ☐ ☐ ☐

5-22g　The DRP system includes the following characteristics:　☐ ☐ ☐ ☐ ☐

1. firm planned orders
2. pegging capabilities
3. customer orders promised for future deliveries in addition to forecasts
4. the ability to include backorders in the netting logic
5. the ability to maintain and change inventory records, location records, and scheduled receipts
6. supplier scheduling in order to provide adequate visibility to outside suppliers
7. rescheduling messages

4—EXCELLENT 3—VERY GOOD 2—FAIR 1—POOR 0—NOT DOING

5-22h The system provides pertinent information for transportation planning in order to be responsive to the needs of the distribution centers as well as to reduce transportation costs. ☐ ☐ ☐ ☐ ☐

5-22i The system provides a shipping schedule that enables cost reductions while at the same time satisfying established loading and shipping needs. ☐ ☐ ☐ ☐ ☐

5-22j Kanban may be used to trigger replenishment from the central supply facility to the distribution centers. ☐ ☐ ☐ ☐ ☐

Appendix A
RECOMMENDED FORMULAS

Over the years, companies have come to us after spending a great deal of time and energy on the best way to calculate the performance measures mentioned in the checklist. For this reason, we've listed the recommended formulas for these calculations in this appendix.

Customer Delivery Performance =

$$\frac{\text{Number of items shipped on time (within quantity and time tolerance)}}{\text{Number of items due (as of original promise date)}}$$

Quality (Parts per Million/Defects per Million Parts*) =

$$\frac{\text{Defects} \times 1{,}000{,}000}{\text{Units processed*}}$$

* Could be shipments, documents, operations, etc.

Cost (Manufacturing Asset Turnover*) =

$$\frac{\text{Annualized cost of goods sold}}{\text{Monthly manufacturing expense} - \text{material purchases}}$$

* Can also use for department or company.

Measures of Velocity =

$$\frac{\text{Value-added time}}{\text{Elapsed time}}$$

Engineering Schedule Performance
(Product Development Activity) =

$$\frac{\text{Number of items received on time}}{\text{Number of items due*}}$$

* User may define timeframe (week, month, etc.).

Production Plan Performance =

$$\frac{\text{Actual production for product family*}}{\text{Planned production for product family*}}$$
(this month) over (planned last month for this month)

* Can be units or a capacity unit of measure such as hours, tons, etc.

Master Production Schedule Performance =

$$\frac{\text{Number of items* completed on time to schedule within tolerance}}{\text{Number of items* due this week based on schedule}}$$
(quantity and time)

* Needs interpretation when scheduling pseudo's, etc.

Manufacturing Schedule Performance =

$$\frac{\text{Number of orders completed on time}}{\text{Number of orders due this week}}$$
(within quantity and time tolerance)

Supplier Delivery Performance =

$$\frac{\text{Number of items received on time} \atop \text{(within quantity and time tolerance)}}{\text{Number of items due this week}}$$

Inventory Record Accuracy =

$$\frac{\text{Number of correct items/quantities/locations*} \atop \text{(within quantity tolerance)}}{\text{Number of items/quantities/locations* checked}}$$

* If discrete location identification is not required, delete from equation.

Bill of Material Accuracy =

$$\frac{\text{Number of correct bills*}}{\text{Total number of bills checked}}$$

* Auditing single-level parent number/component relationships, quantity per, and units of measure.

Routing Accuracy =

$$\frac{\text{Number of correct routings*}}{\text{Total number of routings checked}}$$

* Auditing work center identification, sequence of operations, and standards (within tolerance).

Appendix B

EXAMPLES OF SUPPLEMENTARY PERFORMANCE MEASUREMENTS FOR PLANNING AND CONTROL PROCESSES

In a number of situations, companies have tracked some additional measurements as a way to assess the effectiveness of a particular business function. These supplementary measurements are helpful indicators in assessing how well a particular business function is being accomplished.

SALES AND OPERATIONS PLANNING

1. Sales Plan (actual vs. plan, by family, by month, etc.)
2. Production Plan (actual vs. plan, by family, by month, etc.)
3. Inventory (by product line, finished goods, raw material, work-in-process; by actual dollar level and/or turnover rate vs. current shipment plans, etc.)
4. Customer Service (backorder levels, delivery lead time, number of weeks aging of overdue customer orders, number of involuntary reschedules of customer orders, by product line, etc.)

111

SALES FORECASTING

1. Item accuracy (by week or by month, within preestablished tolerances, by product family, by geographic region, by responsible Sales/Marketing personnel)
2. Family accuracy (within preestablished tolerances, by week or by month, by geographic region, market segment, etc.)

SALES ORDER ENTRY

1. Administrative customer-order promising time (order entry, credit check, document generation, and delivery, etc.)
2. Shipment processing time (custom packaging, crating, loading, shipping, etc.)
3. Percent sales order changes
4. Order-entry accuracy (percentage of orders entered without errors)

MASTER PRODUCTION SCHEDULING

1. Past due (percentage of current output rate, percentage of current in-process aging, etc.)
2. Percentage of schedule changes within near (firm zone) horizon
3. Performance vs. schedule in Finishing/Final Assembly per customer order, where appropriate
4. Linearity of output (by department and to finished goods and/or shipping)

MATERIAL PLANNING AND CONTROL

1. Inventory levels (by planner, by product line, by commodity type vs. seasonally adjusted targets, etc.)
2. Safety stock levels (by planner vs. seasonally adjusted targets, etc.)
3. Material availability (percentage of items available when needed, by week, by planner, by product line, etc.)
4. Planner action/exception messages (percentage of items vs. pre-

established targets, percentage reviewed and acted upon, where appropriate, etc.)

5. Percentage of schedules/orders released with less than planned lead times (by planner, by product line, by supplier, by manufacturing department, etc.)
6. Percentage of schedules/orders rescheduled after release (by planner, by product line, by supplier, by department, etc.)
7. Unplanned activities (material substitutions, product design deviations, by planner, by product line, by department, etc.)

Shop Floor Control, where applicable

8. Percentage of orders/schedules completed on time (by work center/cell/line, by operation, by product line, etc.)
9. Percentage of orders/schedules received on time (by work center/cell/line, by operation, by product line, etc.)
10. Percentage of operations worked out of sequence (by department, work center/cell/line, etc.)
11. Percentage of schedules/orders split after initial release (by department, work center/cell/line, etc.)
12. Work-in-process levels (by work center/cell/line, in equivalent units and/or hours vs. seasonally adjusted targets, etc.)

PURCHASING

1. Percentage of delivery releases with full lead time
2. Percentage of changes to released delivery orders, firm schedules, etc.

CAPACITY PLANNING AND CONTROL

1. Demonstrated capacity (current levels, as compared to planned capacity, by work center/cell/line)
2. Input/output controls (actual input, where applicable, and output hours/units by work center/cell/line vs. targets)
3. Percentage of capacity plans past due (by work center/cell/line)
4. Percentage of schedules/orders routed to alternate work centers or

subcontractors (by product line, by department or work center/cell/ line)

5. Level of overtime work (by department, work center/cell/line vs. seasonally adjusted targets)

6. Work-in-process, manufacturing lead time, and queue levels (by work center/cell/line, in equivalent units and/or hours vs. seasonally adjusted targets, etc.)

7. Percentage of operations worked out of sequence (by department, work center/cell/line, etc.)

8. Percentage of schedules/orders split after initial release (by department, work center/cell/line, etc.)

9. Percentage of schedules/orders received on time (by work center/ cell/line, by operation, by product line, etc.)

BILLS OF MATERIAL

1. Percent of sampled bills correct

2. Percent of item master records correct (includes planning parameters, descriptive data, etc., by planner, by product)

INVENTORY RECORDS

1. Percent of inventory item/locations accurate

2. Percent of work orders accurate (includes checks on actual order quantity and work center location)

ROUTINGS

1. Percent of sampled routings correct

2. Routing change response time

DISTRIBUTION RESOURCE PLANNING

1. Distribution inventory turnover (by distribution center, by product)

2. Freight cost (from manufacturing to distribution centers, distribution center to distribution center transfers, total)